A WESTERN HORSEMAN BOOK

BARREL RACING

Completely Revised

The A.R.T.© (Approach, Rate, Turn)
of Barrel Racing

By Sharon Camarillo

With Cheryl Machin Price

Edited by Roy Jo Sartin
Photographs by Kathy Peth

BARREL RACING
COMPLETELY REVISED

Published by
Western Horseman magazine

3850 North Nevada Ave.
Box 7980
Colorado Springs, CO 80933-7980

www.westernhorseman.com

Design, Typography, and Production
Western Horseman
Colorado Springs, Colorado

Cover photograph by
Kathy Peth

Printing
Publisher's Press
Salt Lake City, Utah

©2000 by Western Horseman
a registered trademark of
Morris Communications Corporation
725 Broadway
Augusta, GA 30901
All rights reserved
Manufactured in the United States of America

Third Printing: August 2002

ISBN 0-911647-56-2

DEDICATION

This book is dedicated to the horses who have so patiently tolerated our growth as riders, and at the same time allowed us the vehicle to be called horsemen. To my friends and colleagues who share my desire to seek and refine skills in a quest to make competition an art form. To my students, who have helped me develop and practice my teaching skills.
To my husband, Leo, and to my children, Storme and Wade, who have shared in the turbulence and reward of competition. To my mother and dad, who remain my greatest and most supportive fans.

ACKNOWLEDGEMENT

To Randy Witte, who helped develop the format and concept behind this book. To Cheryl Machin Price, who shares my passion and interest in instructional horsemanship and whose patience provided the revision of this text. To photographer Kathy Peth and illustrator Dorothy Peth, for their creative interest and determination to create the photos and diagrams necessary for the revision. To Susan Van Rein, for allowing me to borrow her fine horse, Quatro.

Sharon Camarillo

SHARON CAMARILLO

EDITOR'S NOTE

My thanks to *Western Horseman* assistant art director Jeanne Mazerall for the new design of this revision of *Barrel Racing* and to *Western Horseman* associate designer Jessica Butts for re-creating the book's many diagrams and illustrations. And, as always, my gratitude to the entire editorial team at *Western Horseman* for careful proofreading of text and style.

Roy Jo Sartin

ROY JO SARTIN
WH Associate Editor

INTRODUCTION

This book will help you set goals, put a foundation on your horse, and develop your skills as a horseman and competitor.

SHARON CAMARILLO is respected as a consistent winner in barrel racing after competing in the event at four National Finals Rodeos. Her talents as a motivational instructor and clinician have gained her international acclaim.

Sharon has the willingness and ability to help others find success in the popular sport of barrel racing. She emphasizes the importance of traditional horsemanship skills in training the barrel horse to produce consistent performance and to help identify problems and their solutions.

This book contains a formula for success—a package of knowledge she has compiled over the last 20 years through training, competing, and instructing. The goal is to inspire the best of both horse and rider. Sharon has read and studied, asked questions of other professionals in the horse industry, and gradually developed her own successful training and conditioning programs. Her horses stay fresh, willing, and productive.

A four-time National Finals Rodeo qualifier, Sharon Camarillo refers to herself as an eternal student of horsemanship.

"Let's face it," Sharon says, "barrel racing can become very dull for a horse. It's not like working a cow or following cattle in the roping pen. With three stationary objects in the arena the horse can get sour working the same pattern. In order to avoid this resentment, it is important to develop specific skills for training and conditioning that can be accomplished away from the barrels. We don't have to make the task complicated. With a strong foundation, a barrel horse can be guided through the *approach*, collected for the *rate*, and positioned for the *turn*—hence the phrase 'the A.R.T. of barrel racing.'"

Sharon believes a winning edge comes from preparation. This includes a program of training and conditioning at home, and reinforcement of the program during the warm-up period before a barrel run. In this book she explains how to determine when a horse is warmed up and ready to deliver peak performance during a money run.

Sharon introduces the significance of establishing believable and achievable goals and the importance of making positive choices. City-raised and college-educated, Sharon says, "If I can do it, anyone can. It's a matter of wanting something badly enough and sticking to it."

The Sport of Barrel Racing

"As for the future of barrel racing, it's unlimited," says Sharon. "In professional rodeos, prize money now equals that offered in the men's events. Additional opportunities are being created by high-stakes competition for young horses. National organizations have been established to reward entry-level and intermediate riders, and high school and college competitions continue to prepare our youth for the professional ranks."

Barrel racing has come a long way. It began as a way for 1940s rodeo queen contestants to display their riding skills, and gained popularity through all-girl rodeos, small barrel racing associations, and informal "playday" competitions. Early barrel racers rode horses bred for other events, like cutting or roping. There were no specific barrel racing saddles or equipment; no training was known or required. If a horse could really run, or liked to turn, he would probably win the race. In the early stages of the sport, a horse didn't have to be able to run *and* turn to be competitive.

Women competing in the late 1950s laid the groundwork for modern-day barrel racing. Mildred Farris earned 12 National Finals Rodeo qualifications and reserve championships. Wanda Bush won 23 world championships in a variety of events. Sammy Thurman, a world champion barrel racer, added innovations to the event with clinics and products. All three talented cowgirls, in addition to setting the pace for today's competition, offered leadership that provided the groundwork for the formation of the modern Women's Professional Rodeo Association.

"I have to give these women and many more like them credit for their sacrifices and contributions in directing barrel racing toward the sport it is today," Sharon says.

As the barrel race becomes more technical and competitive, the heavy-handed "whip-and-spur" method is being replaced by educated horsemanship. Riders are modifying their styles and training techniques to create more consistent barrel horses who stay willing and enthusiastic for a longer period of time.

Sharon's Philosophy

Longevity requires a multidimensional approach. Knowledge of equine management, including health, conditioning, and nutrition, is critical in the maintenance of the athlete. Development of riding techniques, including balanced seat and intelligent use of aids, is imperative in training. The establishment of a correct foundation through training and conditioning, and the creation of the competi-

Sharon believes that most horse problems are rider-related, and resolving them requires working with the rider first.

Intensifying strengths and strengthening weaknesses are the keys and the challenges.

tive ability that requires precise physical and psychological skills for both the rider and his equine partner, is important.

This "whole horse philosophy" is the method Sharon outlines in this book. The program is designed to put a good foundation on the horse and at the same time train and educate the rider. The horse will acquire a background that will help him reach the height of his ability and a foundation on which a responsible rider can rely when trouble arises. If a horse goes through his training program and just doesn't have the heart or the athletic ability to make a winning barrel horse, he will still be a nicely trained individual who can be used in another discipline.

"Nobody likes a spoiled, sour, uncontrollable horse, and that is what my training program is geared to prevent at all costs," Sharon says. "I emphasize foundation horsemanship principles throughout the book."

Sharon believes that most horse problems are rider-related, and resolving them requires working with the rider first. "Consistency and intelligent handling remain the keys to successful communication with the horse," she says.

Part of successful communication requires an understanding of horse psychology—the natural instincts that govern a horse's responses—and the use of a horse's natural instincts to form a relationship. Communication and establishing mutual

respect between horse and human are essential. Sharon's clinics present the importance of consistent, correct handling as a way to obtain respect from the horse. This is in contrast, she points out, to aggressive techniques, which are often a product of frustration that stems from a lack of rider knowledge and resources.

"Instead of nonproductive anger, riders need to develop patience, and at all times be aware and attentive to the horse's movements and attitudes," she says. "The rider needs to be prepared at any time to make productive corrections, if necessary.

"The plan in training is to be flexible. Being flexible allows the rider to respond with problem-specific corrections at the right time for the right reasons with consistent rewards and discipline. The end goal may be reached in several ways without making a horse feel pressured in a direction that may be too intimidating or too difficult for his individual stage of learning.

"Rider consistency in action is important in making the finished product. You cannot let a horse walk all over you one day and expect him to respect you the next. I also believe it is the rider's responsibility to do everything possible to be a good manager for the horse. I believe this is a multidimensional process that requires the rider to invest intellectually and physically to be the best possible asset to his or her horse.

"This includes creating a support system of equine professionals (including vets and farriers) to act as a 'pit crew.' The rider-trainer needs to be open to continually refining abilities on and off the horse. The rider-trainer also should analyze horse performance and determine whether any problem stems from training or timing, or perhaps is a physical problem with the horse or a problem with the rider.

"Viewing every run as a report card and keeping mistakes in perspective are the challenges. The process of finding the solution determines your ultimate success as a horseman. So, let's begin."

—Cheryl Machin Price

CONTENTS

GOALS

To keep goals in perspective, make them believable and achievable.

EVERYONE NEEDS a goal, something to work toward. I grew up in the city and gained riding experience through summer and weekend outings. When Dad took me to the 1969 National Finals Rodeo in Los Angeles, I could sense my adrenaline rush as the horses' hoofs pounded the arena dirt and the crowd cheered for each rider. I wanted to be a barrel racer!

As I learned more about the sport, I realized I wanted to modify my original goal. I wanted to be recognized as a competent barrel racer by my peers and as a horsewoman outside of the rodeo business. I wanted to change other horsemen's attitudes about the sport. That became my

KENNETH SPRINGER

I always had an interest in the timed event of barrel racing. The more I competed, my focus turned to qualifying for the National Finals Rodeo. This is Seven and I at the 1981 NFR.

KENNETH SPRINGER

My next goal was to become a better horseman. I then realized I could help others achieve the same goals by teaching horsemanship at my barrel racing clinics. These are competitors at the Sharon Camarillo Classic, a contest for students of my clinics.

goal. I began to wonder if there would be a chance to combine the skill and expertise of showing performance horses with the fast pace of barrel racing.

I started to watch, ask questions, experiment, fail, modify, find some success, and refine my knowledge and skills. I wanted to be recognized not only as a horsewoman, but as a scholar and a lady as well. My ultimate goal was to ride well and present a poised and disciplined picture. I believed that when I looked good and when my horse looked good and was working well, I felt more aggressive and confident as a competitor.

My next goal was to become a consistent winner, and then to qualify for the National Finals Rodeo. One of the proudest moments of my life was riding in my first National Finals grand entry alongside my husband, five-time world champion team roper Leo Camarillo.

It takes a lot of drive and determination to qualify for the NFR. To compete for a world championship requires even more drive and determination and is a combination of many sacrifices. It takes a great horse willing to give everything he has. It takes luck, which I believe is where preparation meets opportunity. And perhaps most importantly, it takes a partner—a parent or husband who wants the championship as much as the rider.

I feel it is important to keep goals in perspective, however; they must be believ-

FRANK MARTIN

I reached another goal, to be recognized by my peers as being knowledgeable about both horsemanship and barrel racing, when I became part of the broadcast team at the annual Houston Livestock Show and Rodeo. From left, Bill Bailey, me, Boyd Polhamus, and Bob Tallman.

able and achievable. In order to reach your ultimate goal, you must have a plan that consists of short-, medium-, and long-term achievements. Each phase needs a series of checks and balances, personal rewards, and a time frame for completion. Even your daily activities should have goals that allow you to take a step every day toward your personal success.

My goal with this book is to identify horsemanship as it is applied to the A.R.T. of barrel racing. I want to introduce the important resource of foundation horsemanship, which in turn helps the rider-trainer to become more confident in identifying and correcting specific problems, and helps make competition rewarding at whatever level is chosen.

In order to reach your ultimate goal, you must have a plan with short-, medium-, and long-term achievements.

2 PROSPECTS

When shopping for a prospect, you must consider your skill level, your goals, and your price range.

IN THE quest for a "barrel horse prospect," consider what type of financial commitment is appropriate for your situation. Don't spend a sum that will cause a financial hardship.

Balancing the cost of the horse with the level of competition and availability of prize money is an important consideration. Thought must be given to the resale value of the horse in order to protect your investment if the horse proves unsuitable for your level of ability or competition.

Dollar for dollar, riders in search of barrel horse prospects are in competition with performance horse trainers for cow horse prospects and with race horse people for the top running-bred horses.

A race horse, cow horse, or reining horse prospect who did not excel in his sport for whatever reason can make a barrel horse prospect. A horse may not be suited for one event, but with time and training might be productive in another.

Since barrel futurities accept horses as

A well-balanced horse, like this one, will move more efficiently, thereby reducing stress on joints. A horse who is larger on the front end or higher in the hindquarters tends to travel heavy on the front end, increasing the chance for front-end lameness.

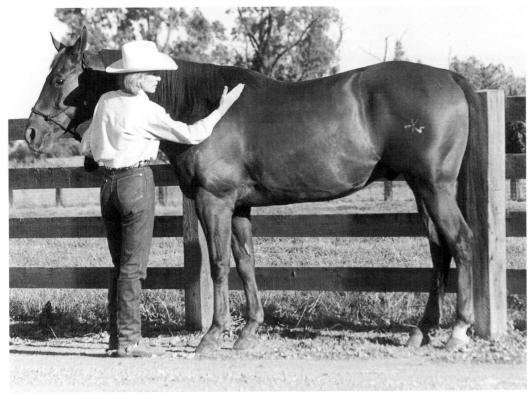

The slope of the hip and shoulder determine the stride, the pushing power, and the strength the horse will have to run and turn.

4- and 5-year-olds, that is another plus in our favor. We might be able to obtain a horse who was shown in another discipline as a 3-year-old, allow him to mature, and perhaps direct him to a barrel futurity as a 4- or 5-year-old. Bottom line: A great horse is a great horse, and usually has the ability to excel in a number of areas.

Few good young horses who excel at futurities go on to make great open horses. Perhaps the young horse has been asked for so much so early that he does not have anything more to give. In some cases a lack of quality foundation does not give the horse the ability to handle the strenuous pressure of open competition. However, because a greater number of horses are currently entering futurities, we are now seeing an increase in the number of horses having successful futurity and open careers.

Such futurity horses include Lynn McKenzie's great horse Magnolia Missle, Kristie Peterson's talented horse Bozo, and Kay Blandford's tremendous horse The Key Grip. Magnolia Missle was a futurity winner who went on to win two WPRA world championships. Caution, however, needs to be taken, because most horses are not ready for the stress of open or pro competition immediately out of futurity ranks.

Attitude

An important aspect in selecting a prospect is that the horse must want to be trained. This is demonstrated by some horses who, in spite of the rider, will go on to perform. The goal is to capitalize on the horse's willingness and desire. This will help ensure that the horse will be marketable in another area if he doesn't prove suitable for barrels.

When considering attitude, the gender of the horse could be a factor. I tend to prefer geldings. In many cases they are easier to haul, and their competitive moods are more consistent than mares or stallions. Personally, geldings are more compatible with my personality. I'll have to say that I have been outrun by some outstanding mares and stallions, but, for

Balance the cost of the horse with the level of competition and availability of prize money.

The front legs support 60 to 65 percent of the horse's body weight, so you want the horse to bear weight evenly on both legs. When the horse stands relaxed, the distance between his front feet should equal the distance between his legs at the chest. The horse has correct alignment when an imaginary line, drawn from the point of the shoulder to the ground, equally divides the front leg.

balance is critical. For example, I do not want a horse who has an extremely large front end in comparison to his hindquarters. I avoid a horse who appears to be "rump high" or runs downhill. A downhill horse tends to be very heavy on the front end, and has difficulty shifting his weight to his hindquarters for quick or collected turns. I look for low hocks and short cannon bones to allow the horse to move quickly and close to the ground.

I want the horse to have a graceful neck and a clean, thin throatlatch in proportion to his body. I do not want an excessively long neck, and I pay attention to how and where the neck attaches to the shoulders. I avoid ewe necks. The ewe neck indicates an excessive curvature at the base of the cervical spine, making it difficult for the horse to elevate the base of his neck in order to achieve good carriage. These horses usually are hollow in the back and have too high a head carriage.

I want the horse to have a strong loin coupling to allow for effective use of his hindquarters. I look for a long underline for the all-important stride. Remember that excessive length in a back sometimes indicates a weak loin. This can cause a training problem because a horse with a weak loin can have a problem rounding his back for collection. A good rule of thumb is no more than a hand's width between the point of the hip and the last rib. Any greater distance could reflect a weakness, which will show up in training and competition.

The slopes of the hip and shoulder determine the stride, the pushing power, and strength the horse will need to run and turn. I look for blemishes like splints, spavins, and windpuffs that may indicate weakness either in conformation or performance. The bone structure should be balanced to the size of the body in order to handle the strain the horse will be under. The hocks and knees should be large (box-like) and flat to help absorb concussion.

the most part, if the horse is used strictly for a rodeo horse, I don't think you can beat the more even-tempered gelding.

Conformation

I look for particular conformation qualities in a barrel horse prospect. Overall

The neck is important in helping the horse to balance. Caution should be taken to avoid ewe-necked horses, who are often also hollow-backed and high-headed.

Attitude, conformation, and pedigree are important, but quality of the individual is key.

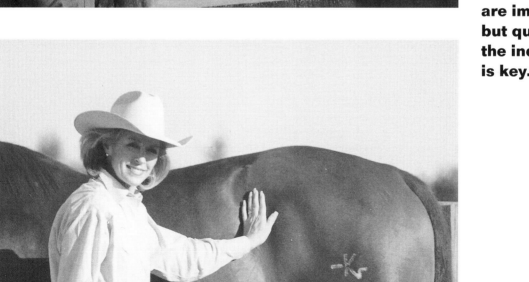

To avoid excessively long-backed horses, a good rule of thumb is no more than a hand-width between the point of the hip and the last rib. This horse's strong loin-coupling gives him effective use of his hindquarters.

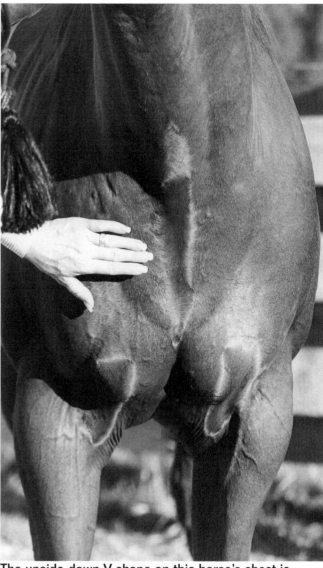

Everyone has preferences for "types" of heads, but consider the horse's ability to eat, breathe, think, and see. This horse displays good distance between his ears and eyes, indicating a good-sized cranium; large nostrils for taking in air; and eyes prominently set on the sides of his head.

The upside-down V-shape on this horse's chest is formed by the pectoral muscles, which help a horse move his legs and elevate his front end. Muscles on the inside and outside of the front legs should taper gradually to the knee.

Consider buying a horse that is proportionate to your size.

We can't ignore the feet. The old saying definitely stands: "No feet, no horse." I want good-sized feet that will aid in circulation and soundness. Heels should be well spread, all connecting to pasterns of good length. Pasterns should slope proportionately to the line in the slope of the shoulder.

As for the head, we can talk about the look in the eye and the size and shape of the nose and nostrils, which enable the horse to suck in plenty of air, but the important part is that the head complements the body. However, I've seen some beautiful athletes with rough, unattractive heads. Sometimes the shape adds to the character of the horse, and after you get acquainted, you wouldn't trade that Roman nose for the prettiest of halter heads!

Like everything else about a winner, size is semi-irrelevant. Theoretically, 15.1 to 15.3 hands is the size I like. A larger horse who needs secure ground to support himself in his turns might have more difficulty with footing on hard or slick ground. However, on heavy ground his size and power can be an advantage. A smaller horse might have difficulty by getting stuck in heavy ground.

The rider should consider buying a prospect that is proportionate to his or her size. I don't like to see a tiny rider overpowered by a disproportionately larger mount, or vice versa. This is a personal observation, and I've certainly appreciated performances by the exceptions to this rule.

What we have to remember, as we search for our ideal horse, is that quality of the individual is what's important. It's true that a well-pedigreed horse will have better selling credentials. But, in the barrel race, the breeding alone offers no guarantee the individual will excel. Of full brothers and sisters, one might make it, and the other might not.

Particular pedigrees do, however, give us an insight into a horse's background and his ability to accept training. There are lines that seem to produce the mental aptitude and athletic performance required in our event. Barrel racing requires a quick, athletic horse who can run. The horse must have a lot of heart and desire and a mind capable of keeping those volatile qualities under control.

Buyer Skills

As a buyer, it is your responsibility to:

- **Identify your own skill level.**
- **Identify your goal.**
- **Identify your price range.**
- **Identify your ability to manage the prospect's level of training.**

Remember: Make sure that the prospect isn't misrepresented by the seller.

Bottom line: Before I commit myself to buying a horse, I consider how the horse handles under saddle. I also watch his natural moves, turned loose without a saddle in a corral. I'll shoo him around and see how he handles his body. I want

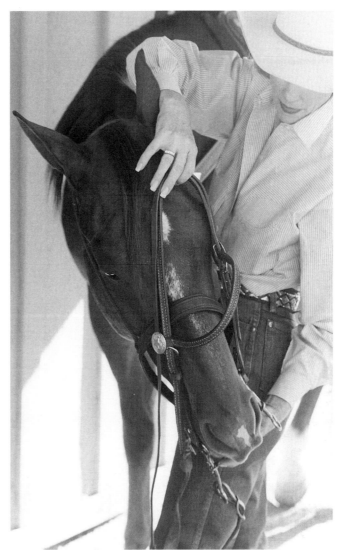

If a prospect is trained, you'll want to take him around the barrels, both in the comfort of his home surroundings and in a competition situation. Saddling and bridling him yourself often reveals bad habits.

to see his hocks well under him when he runs and rolls back. I want to see a free movement in his shoulders and hips. I want to see how close to the ground he travels and if he uses his neck to balance himself.

These are all indications of the horse's athletic ability. Before you purchase, if the horse is ready to go to the barrel pattern, he should be tried out both at home and under the stress of simulated or actual competition. Then a realistic decision can be made if the horse is for you.

Do you feel comfortable and safe with the horse? Be honest and go with your gut feeling. If you don't trust the horse from the beginning, chances are you never will.

3 EQUIPMENT

Your equipment should fit your horse, be of good quality, and serve a purpose.

THE MOST important things to remember about equipment are fit and function. If an item of equipment doesn't serve a purpose, you may not need it, and if it doesn't fit your horse, you need a piece of equipment that does.

That said, it's important to remember that the proper equipment can help you in training your horse and in consistent and successful competition. A good saddle can help you balance on your horse's back, the right bit can help your

Saddle pads made of natural fibers allow "breatheability." Your pad should complement the fit of your saddle, be kept clean to avoid soring your horse's back, and be replaced when worn. It's also good practice for each horse to have his own individual pad.

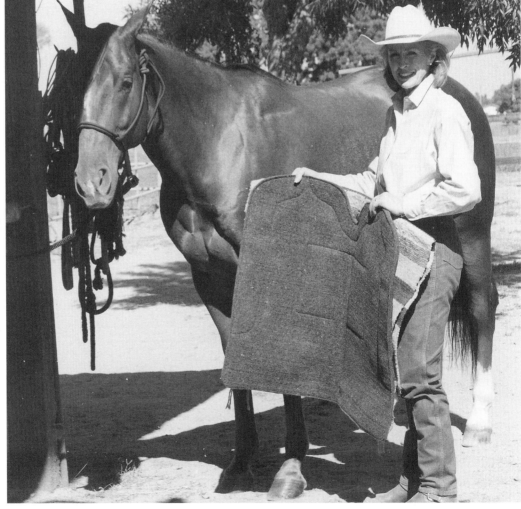

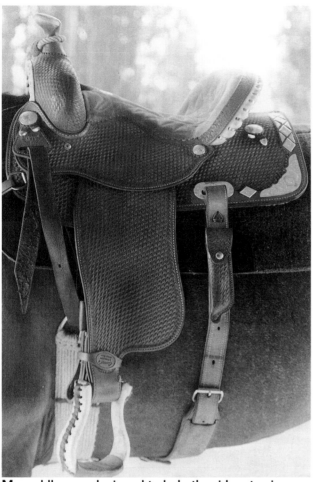

My saddles are designed to help the rider stay in a balanced position. Higher swells and cantle, a flatter ground seat, and the fender and stirrup placement all help the rider stay balanced over the horse's center of gravity.

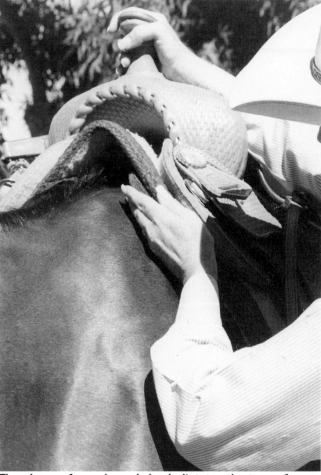

The shape of your horse's back dictates the type of saddle tree he needs. The tree is supposed to bridge laterally over the horse's spine. The saddle should never touch or rub the spine or withers. To assure length of stride and freedom of athletic movement, your horse must have unrestricted movement of his shoulder blades.

horse respond to your cues properly, and protective leg wear can keep leg injuries from sidelining your horse.

However, equipment can't make up for a lack of training, for the horse or for the rider. While you are training or conditioning your horse, train and condition yourself to have good posture, a balanced seat, and light hands. That way, you can make the most of your horse's talents and your good-quality equipment.

Saddles

The most important features of a saddle's design are that it fits the horse and also helps the rider maintain a balanced position. The saddle should help the rider stay in sync with the horse's movements and not sore the horse's back.

I ride a Court's Saddlery Company saddle that I designed and endorse. The ground seat is flatter than that on many saddles, which enables the rider to sit closer to the horse's back. At the same time, the saddle assists the rider in maintaining a balanced position over the horse's center of gravity. The 4-inch cantle also helps the rider stay with a powerful, hard-running, and hard-turning horse. I advise selecting a seat appropriate to the rider's size.

The fenders and stirrups are hung on

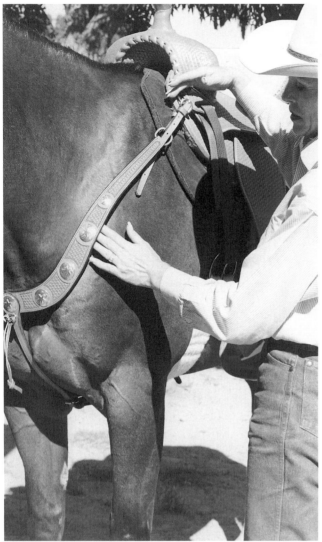

A breast collar helps the saddle stay in position, but should not hinder movement of the shoulder. The small loop of leather attached to the front of the breast collar acts as a keeper for a tie-down strap.

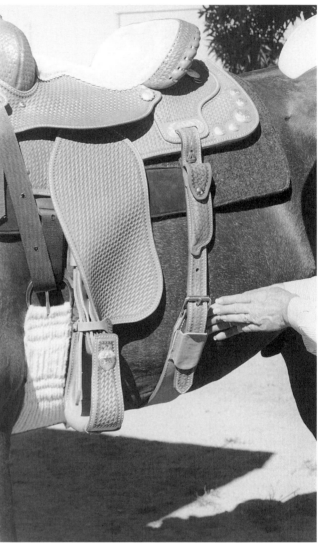

A wide mohair front cinch is great for breatheability and comfort. Adjust your rear cinch snugly to help keep your saddle in place. Always connect the back cinch to the front cinch with a small strap.

the saddle to help maintain good rider position. Proper position can be determined by drawing an imaginary vertical line through the rider's ear, hip, and heel. The fenders and stirrups are hung on my saddle so that the rider's feet and legs hang directly under the hips. The fenders do not allow for much forward or backward motion, and this helps the rider to maintain body position during a run by not letting feet get too far backward or forward.

The 2½-inch bell-bottom stirrups also provide a floor to help balance the rider's feet. The higher, 4-inch cantle helps the rider stay ahead of the horse, and the swells are upright, thus preventing the rider from leaning too far over the horse's front end in an approach and turn. The balance point in this type of saddle makes it easier not to rely on the saddle horn so much to maintain a balanced position.

The shape of your horse's back dictates the type of saddle tree he needs. Start by identifying his back conformation. Is it a Thoroughbred-type with prominent withers and relatively sloping sides? Is it more of an old-fashioned Quarter Horse back with stocky withers and wide sides? Or is it the evolved Quarter Horse-type back, combining heavy muscle with more prominent withers?

Take into account the length of the horse's back and the width and height of the shoulders. The tree should mirror the horse's back as much as possible for the best fit. A key to understanding saddle design is that the tree is supposed to bridge laterally over the horse's spine. The saddle should never touch or rub the spine or withers. The saddle must allow for unrestricted movement of the horse's shoulder blades.

Warning signs that should alert you to problems with saddle fit include small dry spots (quarter-size) on an otherwise wet back after a ride, a back that is sore to the touch, and broken or worn hairs. A horse who switches his tail and lays his ears back when he is saddled or performs poorly under saddle could have a sore back, possibly caused by an ill-fitting saddle.

For saddle pads, I prefer Navajo or felt pads. Pads should complement the fit of the saddle. I look for close contact between my legs and the horse when padding under the bar area.

The saddle should not roll on the horse's back, and to help prevent that from happening, I recommend the use of a breast collar to help keep the saddle in place. As for cinches, a wide mohair front cinch seems hard to beat for horse comfort and a secure fit. A back cinch also helps keep the saddle in place. Correct adjustment of a back cinch is to ride it snug. This requires conditioning the horse to the feel of the back cinch. Always connect the back cinch to the front cinch with a small strap.

The weight of the saddle, breast collar, and cinches is a consideration too. Today's competition is so tight that weight could be a factor that affects time. The difference between my "light" saddle and my "regular" saddle is only eight pounds, but I consider the difference significant. More important than the weight of equipment, however, is the general fitness level of

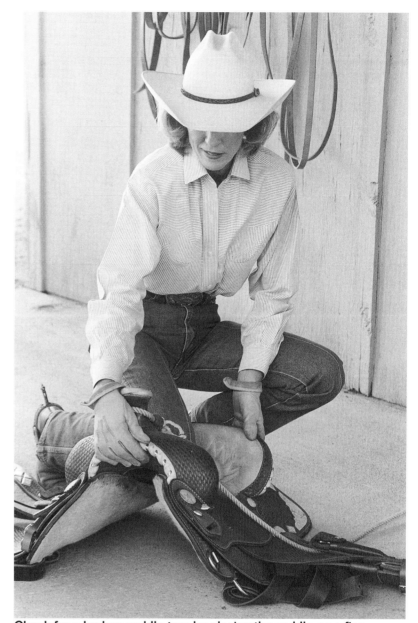

Check for a broken saddle tree by placing the saddle on a firm surface, kneeling on the seat as shown, and pulling up on the pommel and cantle. If the tree is broken, you'll feel the saddle give. Broken trees will sore your horse's back and damage the saddle.

the rider. A fit and balanced rider will be a much greater help to a horse than a lightweight saddle.

Bits

To use any bridle effectively, a rider needs to develop quiet hands that are balanced, soft, and steady on the reins. The rider likewise needs to be aware of the

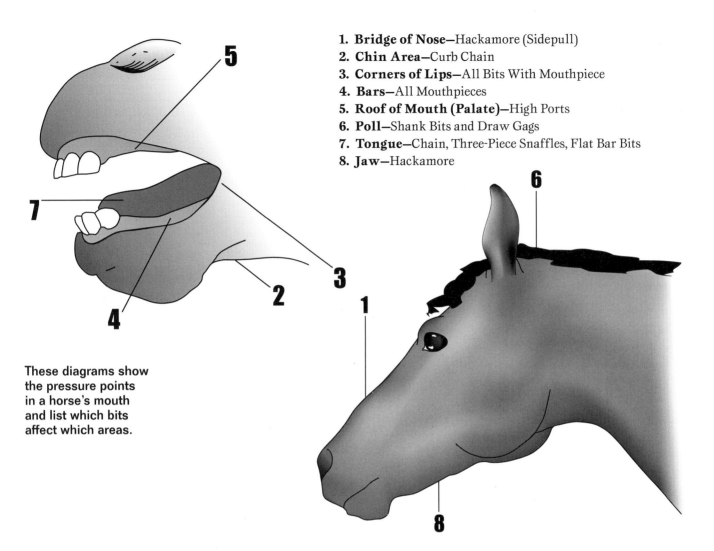

1. **Bridge of Nose**—Hackamore (Sidepull)
2. **Chin Area**—Curb Chain
3. **Corners of Lips**—All Bits With Mouthpiece
4. **Bars**—All Mouthpieces
5. **Roof of Mouth (Palate)**—High Ports
6. **Poll**—Shank Bits and Draw Gags
7. **Tongue**—Chain, Three-Piece Snaffles, Flat Bar Bits
8. **Jaw**—Hackamore

These diagrams show the pressure points in a horse's mouth and list which bits affect which areas.

horse's dental health because freedom from tooth problems is critical to the horse's ability to respond appropriately to the mechanics of any bit. And finally, the rider must understand the process involved in teaching a horse to accept a bit. The horse must understand yielding to pressure and be educated to make a successful transition from a ring snaffle to a bit with shanks and curb.

The diagrams on this page display the pressure points in a horse's mouth and list which bits affect which areas.

I classify bits into three categories: training, transition, and competition.

Training Bits

Training snaffles are designed for teaching a horse to yield to pressure. The ring snaffle works off lip pressure, bar pressure, and tongue pressure.

Depending on the sensitivity of the horse, select a ring snaffle with either a smooth or twisted-wire mouthpiece. A twisted-wire mouthpiece is used for a horse who tends to be heavy in the bridle. The smaller the diameter of the mouthpiece, the greater the severity of the bit. I advise using a mouthpiece the diameter of a pencil.

The Springsteen snaffle introduces the feel of a solid mouthpiece and simulates curb pressure. When using the twisted-wire or Springsteen, be aware of tender spots on the corners of the horse's mouth. If sore areas are evident, a smooth snaffle can be used until the tender spots heal.

Each of these training bits offers direct, lateral control. Teaching the horse the positioning for turning barrels depends

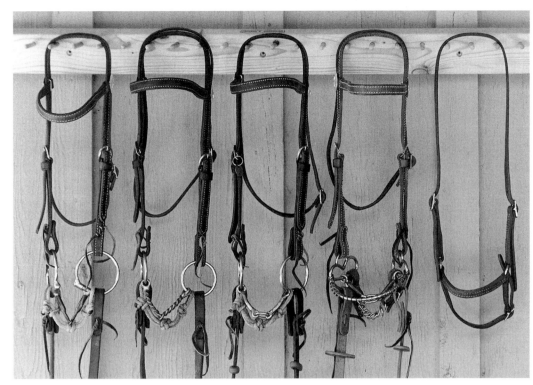

Training snaffles are designed for teaching direct and indirect control. Shown, from left: smooth-mouth D-ring snaffle, twisted-wire O-ring snaffle, three-piece "life-saver" mouthpiece with copper wrap, three-piece "life-saver" mouthpiece with nosepiece, and drop noseband.

on the direct control offered by these bits. A drop noseband should be used on any horse who opens his mouth in an attempt to avoid the snaffle pressure. However, drop nosebands should not be used if the rider does not have responsible hands, for example, if the rider continually yanks and jerks on the reins.

Martingales

Depending on the individual horse's needs, the rider can use a running, poll, or German martingale as an additional training aid. Each of the martingales requires accurate adjustment and is designed to complement the effectiveness of the training snaffles.

The running martingale, when properly adjusted, is the most "neutral" of the martingales. It is designed to be passive unless the horse throws his head up and out of position. Perhaps most importantly, a running martingale can assist with inconsistencies in the rider's hands.

To determine the correct adjustment for the running martingale, lengthen the

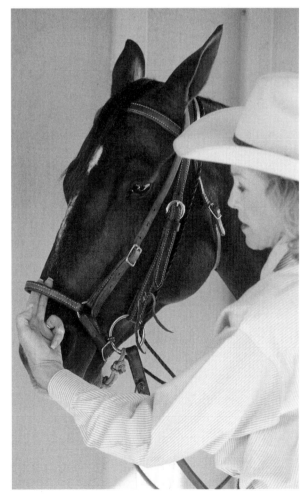

A drop noseband can be used on a horse who opens his mouth to avoid pressure from the training snaffle. But first make sure the rider's hands are not responsible for the problem. Then adjust the noseband so two fingers can be inserted between it and the horse's nose. Place the drop noseband underneath the bit, to avoid pinching the corners of the mouth.

This running martingale is adjusted too short, creating too much tuck. This causes the horse to drop his weight forward, which can create many problems, including imbalanced stops and turns.

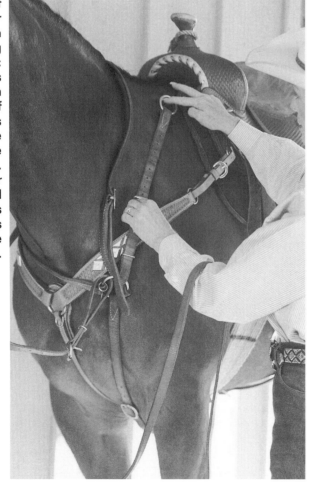

My rule of thumb for adjusting a running martingale: The rings should touch the top of the horse's shoulder blade or the throatlatch. This allows for a direct pull of the reins from the rider's hands to the horse's mouth.

straps until the rings touch the top of the horse's shoulder blade or the throatlatch of the bridle. If the martingale is adjusted too short, the downward pull restricts the horse's forward motion and directs the horse's weight on his forehand; he'll have difficulty balancing in his stops and will turn with his chin tucked to his chest. **Important:** Use "rein stops" to prevent the rings of the martingale from getting hooked on the fittings at the end of the reins, next to the bit.

The poll martingale is effective on a horse who tends to be heavy on the forehand. It can also help teach the horse to rate and stop; it encourages him to keep his hindquarters under him by limbering the loin and restricting the forward movement of the horse's nose. The poll martingale is constructed with a snap and approximately 10 feet of nylon cord.

Attach the snap to the ring on the front cinch, then thread the end of the martingale up from the inside to the outside of the left ring of the snaffle. Place the cord over the horse's poll and thread from the outside to the inside of the right ring. Tie a no-slip knot approximately 12

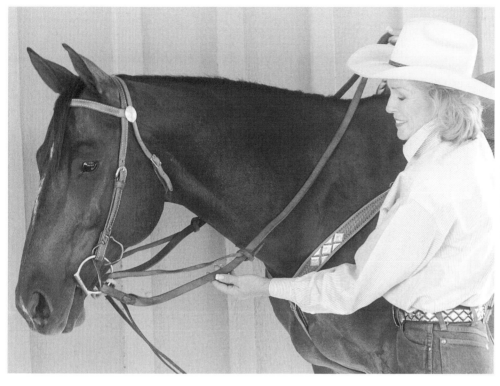

A German martingale helps a horse get collected. This martingale is attached to the front cinch between the horse's legs; its ends run through the D-rings of this snaffle from the inside to the outside, where they're attached to the reins. The "bubble" in the reins ensures that the martingale will take hold before normal rein pressure. Again, do not adjust the martingale too short, which creates an overtucked position.

inches from the throatlatch. The length should allow for a neutral adjustment.

To determine a neutral adjustment, lift up on the martingale. There should be enough length to allow the cord to touch the horse's throatlatch. The horse should not be mounted until he is made to move forward in this martingale. Make sure the horse is not intimidated by the poll martingale before stepping on. Make sure your no-slip knot is correct.

The German martingale helps a horse to learn collection. The German martingale encourages the horse to carry his head at an acceptable position, while rounding his back. It comes into effect only if the horse hollows his back, pushes through the bit, or raises his head. The German martingale is attached to the front cinch, and the straps are brought between the front legs and threaded through the respective bit rings before being attached to the reins.

Be careful to not adjust this martingale too tightly or overtuck the horse's head. Martingales adjusted too tightly can cause a horse to resist harder in an effort to relieve the excessive downward pres-

sure. Too tight a German martingale can teach a horse to overtuck and remain heavy on the forehand.

An improperly selected or incorrectly adjusted martingale, of any type, can be extremely damaging to the training process.

Transition Bits

Once a horse has progressed to the point where he is responsive to the snaffle, it is time to introduce a transition bit. This may be one of the most important aspects of a horse's training.

As discussed previously, the Springsteen can begin this process. The next progression can be to a bit with gag action, shanks, and a curb strap.

A loose-sided bit with a snaffle or ported mouthpiece offers little intimidation to the horse and provides understandable transition in the bitting process. My Tender Touch bits, which have slight gag action, are examples of bits in the transition category. Once the horse is comfortable with the newly introduced pressure points used by the

Training bits offer direct, lateral control; transition bits introduce new pressure points.

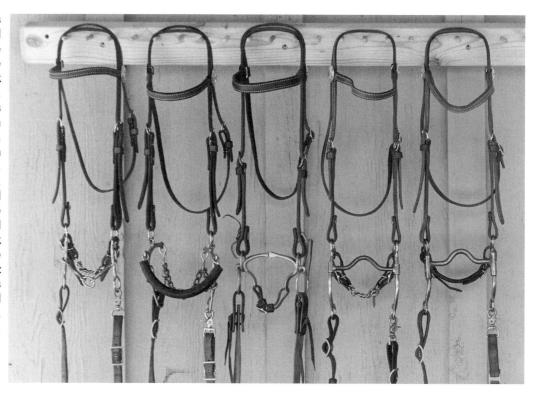

Transition bits introduce curb and indirect pressure through the leverage created by the shank and purchase. Shown, from left: Sharon's Tender Touch three-piece snaffle, short-shanked ultra (snaffle with nosepiece), Springsteen snaffle, transition curb, and swivel curb. These bits can be ordered from many tack catalogs. The Camarillo bit collection is manufactured by Reinsman, 423-559-8799.

A finished barrel horse needs a bit for conditioning and another for competition.

transition bits, consideration of a competitive bit can begin.

The transition stage of training is highly overlooked. Without a successful transition from snaffle to shanked bridles, it can be very difficult to progress into competitive equipment.

Competition Bits

By the time your horse reaches this level, he should understand the pressure being applied by the shank and curb. He is developing a style that is comfortable for him on the barrel pattern, and control at speed is now a consideration. The goal then becomes selecting a bit that will enable you to communicate precisely and efficiently with him during a competitive run.

A finished barrel horse needs two types of bits: one for conditioning and tuning and another for effective control at speed. The horse may be ridden daily in a gag, curb, or training snaffle, whichever seems best suited for him. However, when the horse is in competition, select

a bit that gives you the control needed to handle and balance your horse's speed.

The horse should not be worked in the competition bit unless a correction is necessary. Once he has been corrected, the bit should be taken off and used only for competition. This preserves the effective control of and respect for the competition bit. Riders must respect the control they gain with the competition bit, and not be afraid to change or adjust if necessary to preserve control. Also pay attention to your body position and consistent cues. Any time a horse starts resisting, check for dental problems or worn spots on bits that may cause damage to the horse's mouth.

I categorize competition bits by their effects on the elements of the barrel race—the approach, rate, and turn. You can determine which category of competition bit is most effective for your horse by deciding whether he needs assistance in his approach, rate, or turn during competition. The photos display each category of bit.

With any of the bits, it is important that you understand the control the bit offers. For example, problems in the

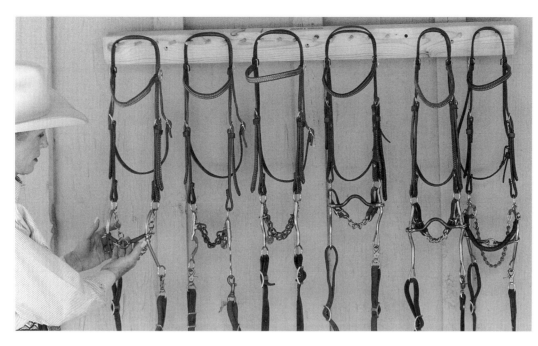

Competition bits in the *approach* category offer the rider increased shoulder control through leverage from the shank and purchase ratio. Shown, from left: three-piece gag, swivel chain, chain, short-shanked lifter, long-shanked lifter, and correction (three-piece snaffle with nosepiece).

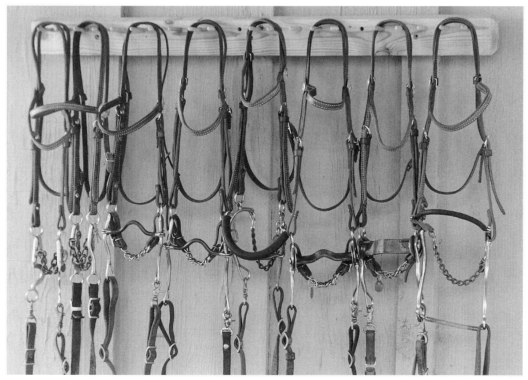

Competition bits in the *rate* category offer the rider increased vertical control to help obtain precise rate and shortening of stride. Shown, from left: swivel chain, chain, short-shanked lifter, long-shanked lifter, long-shanked ultra, swivel polo, polo (these polo bits are also known as Rutledge Roper bits), and hackamore bit.

approach usually relate to problems in maintaining balance and control of the horse's shoulders. Bits that enhance shoulder control are the lifter and combination. Problems in rate can often be addressed by bits that fall into the polo, combination, ported curb, or chain category, for more effective collection and stopping control. Problems in the turn can be assisted by bits that offer some gag action, such as the ultra, Tender Touch, or gag, for more lateral control.

Horses are individuals, and for that reason no bit or bridle should be ruled out. However, allowing a horse to learn he can get away from the rider's control

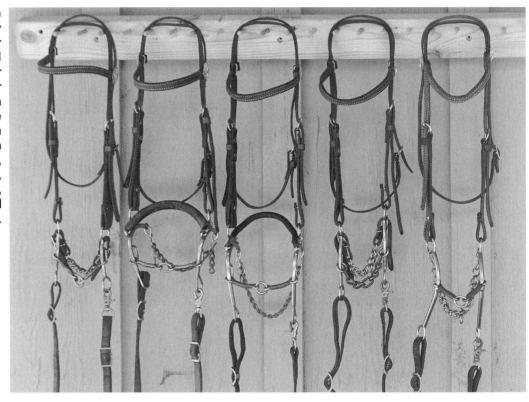

Competition bits in the *turn* category offer the rider increased lateral control for either decreasing or increasing a horse's bend in the turn. Shown, from left: Tender Touch three-piece snaffle, short-shanked ultra, long-shanked ultra, chain, and three-piece gag.

The horse must understand yielding to pressure to make a successful transition from a ring snaffle to a bit with shanks and curb.

is a severe problem. Do not sacrifice control and accuracy for speed. Make sure you have the correct bit to enhance your horse's performance.

Tie-Downs

The term tie-down can be misleading. It should not be used as much to tie the horse's head down as to help him balance in his rate and turns. The tie-down also complements the effectiveness of the competition bridle. There are two major categories of tie-downs—the noseband tie-down and the browband tie-down.

An average adjustment is measured this way: With the tie-down in place, take your hand and see if there is enough slack in the tie-down strap to push it upwards, so it just touches the throat-latch on the horse. This length should help the horse have the collection necessary for a quick turn. Shortening the tie-down strap increases its severity and may shorten a horse's stride.

The noseband tie-down can be made from a variety of materials. The leather noseband gives with the movement of the horse and is the least aggressive. The firmer the tie-down material and the shorter the adjustment, the more severe the control.

The browband tie-down applies pressure to the horse's brow just above the eyes. This encourages the horse to maintain position and discourages extreme elevation of the poll. It works well on a horse who likes to run with his nose out, but does not push through the bridle.

Either tie-down should be properly fitted, and the horse should be allowed to acquaint himself with its effects prior to the rider mounting. It is my observation that the majority of horses I see competing with no tie-down would be more consistent with the addition of some type of tie-down.

Protective Gear

I recommend the use of three pieces of protective equipment: bell boots, com-

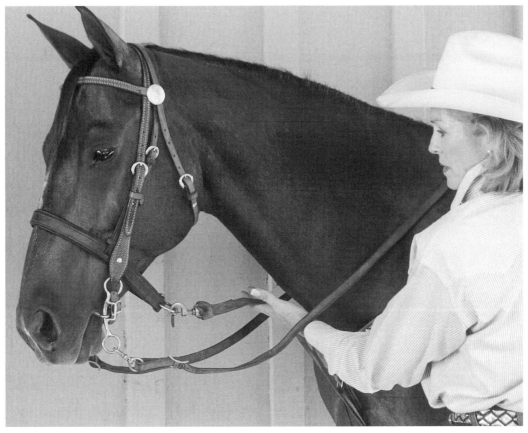

A tie-down helps a horse balance in his rate and turns. This leather noseband tie-down, shown with a neutral adjustment, will give slightly with the movement of the horse. A too-short tie-down strap could cause the horse to shorten his stride and interfere with his natural movement.

The browband tie-down, shown here with a neutral adjustment, allows the horse to lead with his nose while utilizing the tie-down for collection and balance.

Bell boots protect the front feet from overreaching by the hind feet, especially in mud and bad ground conditions.

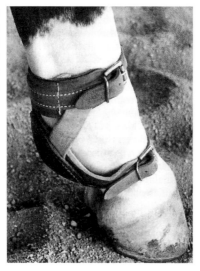

Skid boots protect the hind fetlocks from rough ground in a stop.

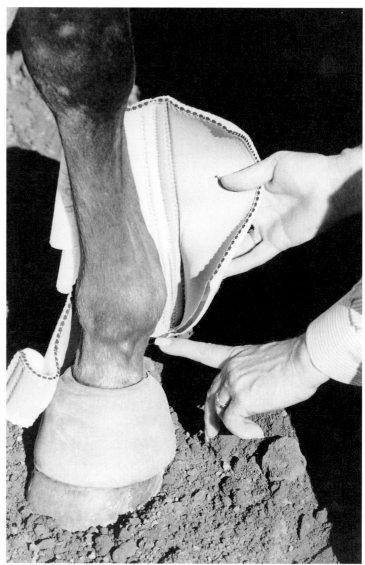

Combination boots protect the splint and fetlock area. If the boot has tendon supports, be sure the boot is aligned properly. Consult the manufacturer's instructions for proper application.

I recommend bell boots, combination boots, and skid boots as protective gear.

bination boots (that offer splint and fetlock protection) for the front legs, and skid boots for the back legs. This gear serves as preventive medicine—it helps guard against injuries. The front feet and legs need protection from interfering and overreaching. The hind fetlocks should be protected from rough ground in a stop.

Some horses might need additional protection. For example, a horse might get "speed cuts," caused by a front foot clipping on the inside of a back leg during a run, or the hind legs might clip one another in a turn. Any time a horse overreaches or clips himself consistently, consult a horseshoer, as the possibility of an imbalance exists.

Bell boots, also known as overreach boots, are most needed in mud and bad ground conditions, where a horse might slip and step on himself.

For a combination boot, the soft nylon varieties with the padded reinforcement in the fetlock and splint areas are preferable. If the horse does not have special problems behind, the standard roper, neoprene skid boots are my choice.

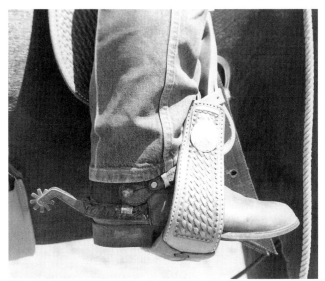
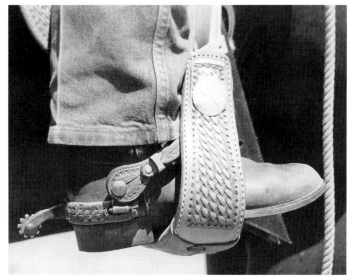

Spurs should be used only by responsible riders who know where their spurs are at all times. Downward-sloping shanks help keep the spur out of the horse's sides and are not as severe as longer, straighter shanks.

I do not suggest using these types of protective gear when just going out for a casual ride. But any arena work at speed requires protective gear. Young horses should wear protective front boots when being worked. This prevents injuries caused by the young horse over-reaching when first learning how to place his feet.

Additional Aids

An over-and-under attached to the saddle horn should not extend down past the horse's knee. Position the over-and-under across your leg before a run, so that you can slide your hand two-thirds of the way down the rope to use it in a quick whipping motion—left side, right side. It is a useful tool to reinforce a request to the horse to move forward if he hesitates. The over-and-under is not as precise as a bat in some instances.

Spurs are used for positioning the horse's body and should not be overused when asking for speed. In fact, in many cases, the use of spurs during a competitive run can be more damaging to a horse's performance than beneficial. It takes a responsible and balanced rider not to misuse a spur in high-speed competition.

The over-and-under, a piece of nylon or leather attached to the saddlehorn and extending down to the horse's knee, is useful in reinforcing a request to the horse to move forward.

ESTABLISHING A FOUNDATION

The basic education of your horse consists of skill-building exercises taught in a round pen and under saddle.

A FOUNDATION must be established before introducing a horse to a cloverleaf barrel pattern. A horse with a well-established foundation should display a trust and willingness to submit to the rider's requests. He understands how to respond to rein pressure and leg aids. The horse can be ridden in straight lines and even-sized circles, and can stop on request. The horse should be solid in his walk, trot, and lope and be able to pick up the correct lead when asked. The horse's ability to be attentive to and remain focused on the rider is mandatory.

Being able to position the horse any place, any speed, any time is the essential element that leads to consistent performance. Though barrel racing appears to be a semi-out-of-control event, the key word is "semi." To develop the skills and

Both you and your horse need a good foundation in horsemanship basics before you head to the barrel pattern.

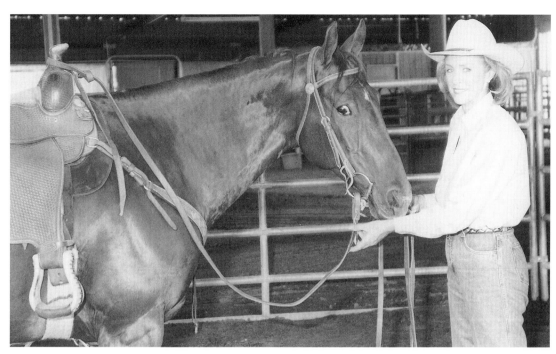

Checking to the tail: You'll need your horse saddled and bridled in a ring snaffle with split reins. Tie the off rein to the saddle horn with no tension and plenty of slack between the horn and bit.

abilities required to compete in barrel racing, the horse must master lessons in the round pen and be proficient in a series of skill-building exercises.

Mastering the following skill exercises will also help you develop a feel for any difficulties or resistance your horse may have before adding the pressure of the barrel pattern. If your horse cannot be properly balanced or framed while performing the skill exercises, he will not be properly balanced during the execution of a barrel pattern.

A foundation based on principles of tried-and-true horsemanship—that is consistently reinforced during the horse's riding and competitive career—allows the rider a positive resource to create a productive and consistent finished product.

We'll approach each of the following exercises with these steps:

- **Application** of the exercise in regards to the A.R.T. (approach, rate, turn) of barrel racing.
- **Goals** for the exercise.
- **Mechanics** of the exercise.
- **Problems** and difficulties encountered in completing the exercise.
- **Plans** to overcome these problems.

Checking

You can determine a horse's level of understanding and confidence by evaluating his willingness and response in a round pen. Checking a horse (also known as "bitting-up" a horse) in a round pen is a mechanical way to teach the horse to yield to rein pressure. The reins can be attached to various parts of the saddle and horse depending on the response desired. Initial checking of a horse is done with snaffle bit and split reins. The horse can be checked to the tail, saddle horn, or cantle of the saddle.

Before you start work, make sure your round pen (or, as a substitute, a 20x20 or larger square pen) is safe, with no protruding objects the horse can rub or catch equipment on. The ground should provide solid, safe, secure footing. The round pen should be large enough to allow the horse to move and act out any resistance without risking injury. Check the condition of the round pen every day. Safety is always the No. 1 consideration. Avoid wire pens!

Note: It is important to remember these exercises are based on education, not discipline. They should not be overdone and should be well-supervised by an experienced horseman knowledgeable in this

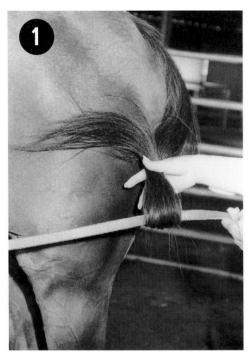

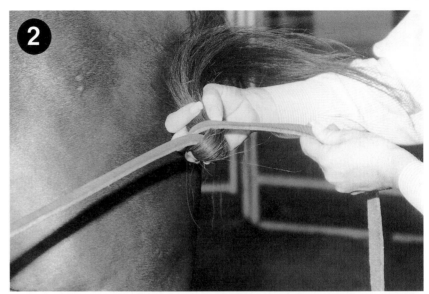

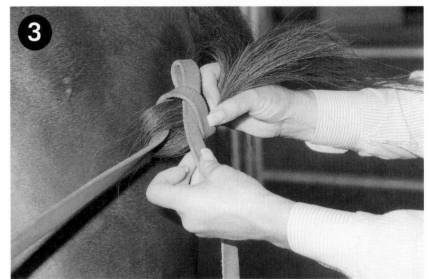

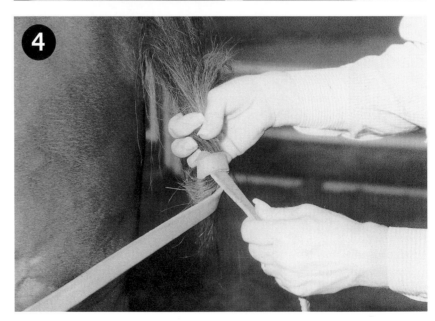

Checking to the tail: Run the other rein through the stirrup and secure to the horse's tail, as shown in these four photos.

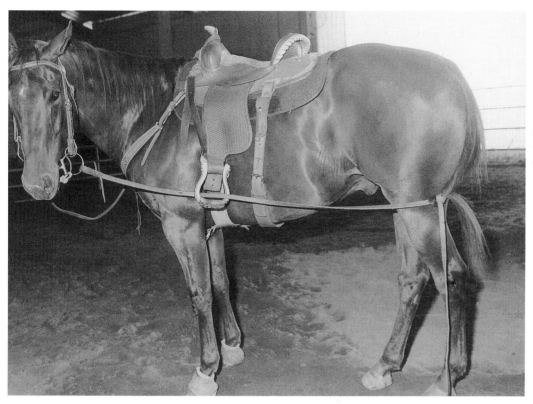

Checking to the tail: Once knot is secure, step away from the horse. Watch him closely to make sure he is not frightened by the rein touching his hind leg. Remember not to tie the rein so tightly that the horse cannot yield to—and thereby relieve—the pressure.

form of education. If the horse is checked too tightly, it could destroy his incentive to respond because he can find no relief from bit pressure. If overdone, the exercises could allow a horse to become too limber, or, even worse, allow him to find his own, unacceptable way to escape the bit pressure.

Checking a horse to his tail or to the cantle of the saddle teaches the horse to yield to rein pressure. It is the prerequisite step for all the following exercises. It lets the horse learn that the pressure is released when he gives or yields toward the pressure.

Application: Checking helps develop the horse's ability to create a bend in the spine. This ability will be required in *turning* around a barrel and accomplishing the following exercises.

Mechanics
- Saddle your horse; then bridle him with a snaffle bit and split reins at least eight feet long. Do not use a cavesson, drop noseband, or martingale.
- Take the saddled horse into the round pen or corral.

- Secure the off rein to the saddle horn with plenty of slack between the saddle horn and bit.
- Run the other rein through the stirrup, and then tie the rein to the tail. Do not tie so short that the horse can't reward himself with release of the rein pressure.
- Be very cautious the first time you release the tail with the rein attached. A horse can be frightened by the rein against his leg or by having his head tied around. You should accustom him to the feel of a rein or rope around his legs before you ever bit him up.
- Move away. Let the horse figure out how to relieve the pressure of the bit on his own.
- Turning your body away from the horse removes eye contact and rider presence.
- As the horse relaxes and begins to give to the rein pressure, approach and stand next to him.
- Ask the horse to move around the pen. Firmly pat the horse on the shoulder and/or hindquarters, if needed, to get him moving in a forward motion.
- Make sure the horse is moving in front

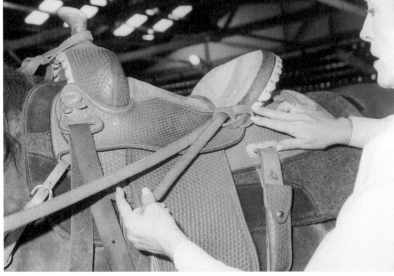

Checking to the cantle: Instead of tying the rein to the tail, you can run the rein across the saddle's seat, looping it around the cantle and tying it to itself, as shown.

and back. He must not plant his front feet and walk his hindquarters, or plant his hindquarters and walk around solely with his front end. The horse must step his front end out of the way so his hindquarters have a place to move up into a forward-moving position.

- The circle needs to show forward movement as the horse moves his front legs and reaches up with his inside hind leg.
- **Caution:** A little checking goes a long way. Rule of thumb: 5-15 minutes, three times a week.

Problem: The problem most likely to occur is that the rider is not familiar with how to work a horse in a round pen. The rider must resist asking for too much too soon and allow the horse to establish confidence and realize the importance of forward motion as he learns to give to pressure and move forward into the bit.

Plan: To resolve this problem, obtain assistance or supervision from an experienced horseman, skilled in this type of education.

Additional checking exercises reflect similar application and goals. The mechanics of the exercises are shown in the "Checking" photos in this chapter.

Skill Exercises

To be ready to be introduced to barrels, a horse needs to be supple, straight, and strong. The following skill exercises help teach, condition, and strengthen the skills the horse will use in barrel racing.

Although these exercises are used for training in the early stages, they can also help tune and maintain balance on a

Checking, moving off: With the horse checked to either the tail or the cantle, step to his hip and ask him to move forward. When the saddle offsets, he's moving with a good arc in his spine.

Checking, moving off: Make sure the horse is moving his front and back legs forward, and not pivoting. Then step back and let him figure out how to relieve the pressure of the bit on his own.

Checking through the front legs: With the reins run between the front legs and attached to a loop of inner tube across the saddle seat, the horse learns to yield to bit pressure from both reins, flexing at the poll.

Backing from the ground: This exercise helps the horse shift his weight to his hindquarters. First knot the reins behind the cantle.

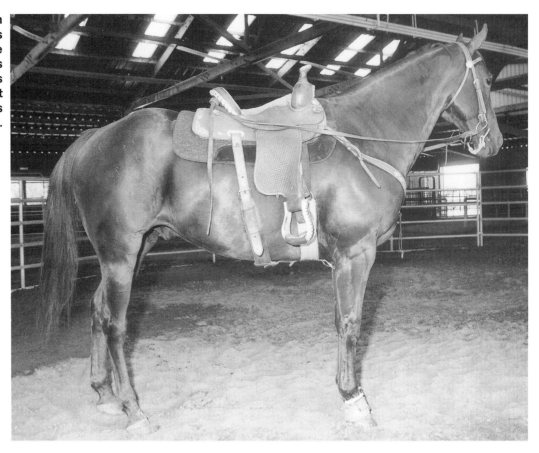

Backing from the ground: Stand alongside the cantle. Pick up the reins and apply gentle pressure to ask the horse to move backward. Release the reins as soon as the horse responds, with a weight shift or small step backwards.

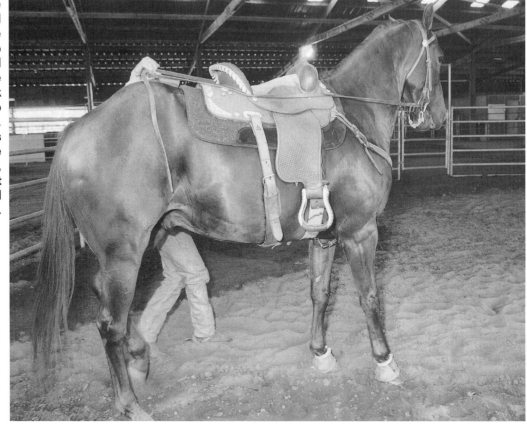

Checking to introduce new bit: You can introduce a new bit by checking to the saddle horn. Use the round pen to introduce a new bit or bridle change. The horse can experiment with new pressure points without the complication of a rider on his back.

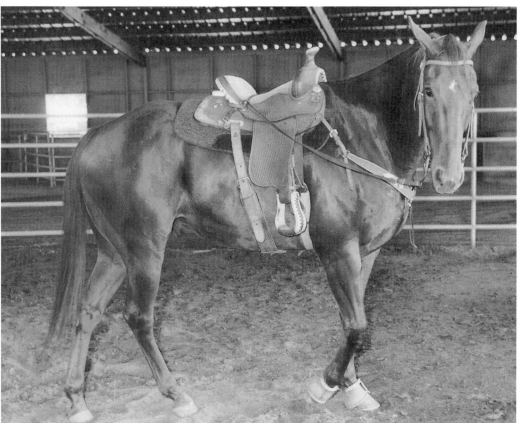

Checking in competition bridle: Checking a horse in his competition bridle can be used on a seasoned horse to lighten his response. Check to the cantle as shown.

Rider hand position is key in communicating effectively with the horse. With your elbows close to your waist, position your hands hip-width apart just in front of your saddle. Use a secure, yet sensitive, grip on the reins.

Always reward your horse's efforts to respond to your cues by releasing pressure on the reins.

solid, seasoned horse as well. These exercises are most productive with a training bridle, such as a ring snaffle with split reins. This offers the rider the direct control necessary to school the horse without the interference of a shank. In general, when positioning the reins, make sure there is plenty of room between your left and right hands so one rein does not inhibit the movement of the other.

It is your responsibility to assess your horse's educational needs. Identify which skill exercises will strengthen your horse's weaknesses and reinforce his strong points. Mixing up the exercises according to your horse's strengths and weaknesses—interspersing work on problem areas with exercises that he can easily master—will help horse and rider develop a positive and confident attitude in training.

Exercise sessions can be done in short periods of time, perhaps eight to fifteen minutes of concentrated work. The equine attention span is different from that of humans. Some horses can take more work; some can't take as much. Identify the mental aptitude of your horse and determine the amount of time appropriate to spend on each task. Watch and learn from your horse's responses. Remember that a horse can get sour from working too long on something he

already does well or understands.

Avoid doing all the skill exercises in one session or repeating them too often. Nothing kills a horse's desire like fatigue or boredom. For example, too many lead changes, limbering exercises, or stops, and a horse becomes resentful instead of responsive. Some horses will use creative resources to cheat or tune out their riders. That lack of attention directly reduces the effectiveness of the training program.

Both horse and rider should be able to ride a perfect circle and to understand leads and diagonals before moving on to the skill exercises.

Visualizing a Circle

As a rider, plan and visualize each exercise so you can help your horse complete the training exercise. You'll also need to be able to correctly apply rein and leg aids at the proper times.

Visual reference points around your riding area can help you. I like to use a lettering or numbering system similar to those seen in dressage arenas. In this way I can direct myself or a student to precise locations during an exercise. You can buy professionally done dressage letters or make your own with spray paint and stencils. You can also use cones or similar objects as landmarks for your riding area.

Prior to starting any pattern work, you and your horse should be able to ride a large, round circle. The circle should utilize up to half of the riding area. Ironically, two of the hardest maneuvers to accomplish precisely are riding a horse in a straight line and in a perfect circle. To perform either requires a combination of rein and leg skills and the ability to identify stiffness and lack of impulsion. The lack of this ability will make it very difficult to place a horse on a barrel pattern.

To ride a perfect circle, establish the size of the circle by looking ahead. In the circle, avoid pulling on the inside rein or carrying the horse's nose to the inside, which creates excess bend in his neck and an imbalanced shoulder. Instead, support both sides of his body with even rein pressure to maintain control of his hindquarters and achieve a balanced frame. His hips/shoulders should not be carried either inside or outside the circle. Think about the circle consisting of four points, like a square, and then look and ride to each point to help maneuver an even, balanced circle, with no flat sides.

Leads and Diagonals

Some of the skill-building exercises are completed with the horse in a lope on the correct lead. Both the horse's and the rider's position create the departure into the lope on the correct lead.

Part of the correct rider position that helps the horse achieve the correct lead is the diagonal. Your understanding of the sequence of the horse's hoofbeats and the rhythm of the trot will help you identify diagonals. In the trot the horse's legs move in alternate diagonal pairs. The two-beat rhythm this creates is separated by a moment of suspension when all four legs are off the ground.

To "post the diagonal," rise and sit in time with the horse's outside shoulder. Rise slightly out of the saddle when the

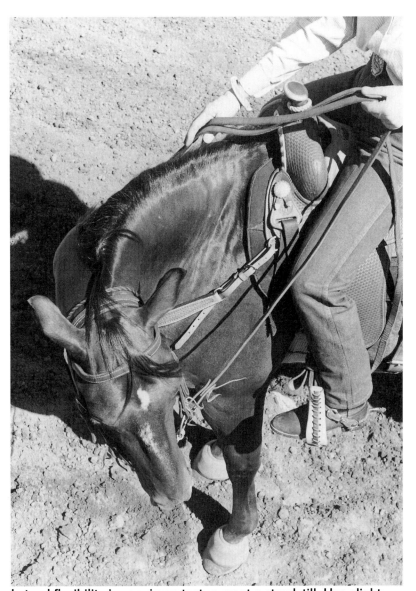

Lateral flexibility is very important, even at a standstill. Use slight rein pressure to direct the horse's nose to the degree you request. Your horse will flex more easily over time.

horse's outside shoulder rises, and sit when the outside foreleg hits the ground.

Check frequently to make sure you're on the correct diagonal. An easy way to change diagonals is to stay in the saddle an extra stride and then return to rising. Correct diagonals help the horse with his own balance and in obtaining correct leads, both of which are required skills for the following exercises and eventually the barrels.

The term *lead* is used to identify which foreleg is leading during a stride at the lope, a gait in which the horse's hoofs

One way to obtain a lead: Trot in a circle, posting on the correct (outside) diagonal. Pick up your outside rein to direct the nose to the outside of the circle; this moves the shoulder to the inside of the circle, pointing the shoulder to the lead. Press your outside leg behind the cinch to cue the horse's hindquarters to step to the inside and lope off. If you're trotting a circle to the right, as shown, your horse should lope off in the right lead.

This elementary method has proven most effective for my students:

- With the horse trotting in a circle, post on the correct diagonal. Remember the rule: Rise and fall with leg on wall.
- With the outside rein (the rein to the outside of the circle), direct the horse's nose slightly to the outside of the circle. As a result, the horse's inside shoulder will move slightly to the inside of the circle.
- Apply pressure behind the cinch with your outside leg, which cues the horse to lope.

The combination of the horse's and rider's position creates the departure into the lope on the correct lead. If a horse is moving in a circle to the left, he should pick up the left lead; if he is moving in a circle to the right, he should pick up the right lead. If the horse fails to take the correct lead, or takes the correct lead in front, but not with the hind legs (this is called cross-firing and results in a very rough, uncoordinated lope), then you should drop the horse to a trot and repeat the sequence. This procedure provides consistency in obtaining the correct lead both on and off the barrel pattern.

The Corkscrew

This exercise begins by loping a balanced, even circle, at least 50 feet in diameter. When the horse and rider are framed and balanced, they begin a series of gradually smaller circles (smaller by five- or ten-foot increments) in a spiraling-down formation, until they reach the center of the "corkscrew." More advanced horses can maintain an even, balanced gait in a very small circle (six to ten feet) at the corkscrew's "eye," or center. Then the rider drops the horse down to a trot, maintains this small circle at a trot until the horse relaxes, picks up the lope on the other lead, and begins the exercise from a large circle in the opposite direction.

Application: Because of the difficulty of rider and horse performing a precisely

create a three-beat rhythm. A horse lopes on the right lead when the right foreleg stretches farther out than the left foreleg during a stride, and vice versa.

Balance depends on the horse's ability to maintain a correct lead both in the skill-building exercises and later in the barrel pattern. It is essential for your horse's education that you can identify and cue for the correct lead. You can use various methods to obtain a correct lead; choose a method that both you and your horse understand.

Posting the diagonal: As the horse trots, I rise slightly out of the saddle when the horse raises his outside (here, the left) foreleg, and I sit as that leg hits the ground, posting on the correct diagonal.

placed circle, this is probably the most important exercise used throughout every phase of a horse's training. It is good to use on a young or green horse just starting out, provided you do not force him into too tight of a circle at first. Follow your horse's pace and build his confidence. Establish a size of circle he can comfortably maintain at a lope in the correct lead.

This exercise can benefit a high-strung horse who needs to be ridden down and relaxed. It also aids an older horse in keeping his spine supple. This exercise helps horses with their leads, reinforces their body suppleness, and encourages them to work off their hocks—all movements needed to run barrels.

The corkscrew is also a great warm-up and can be used to help condition a barrel horse when outside riding is not available. A 10-minute gallop is an extensive workout. Two to three direction changes are usually sufficient. Work the corkscrew at a variety of speeds. This allows the horse to be introduced to speed without getting excited or intimidated.

Goal: To produce a horse who can complete a corkscrew at a variety of speeds, in perfect and precise circles. The horse should remain relaxed in the corkscrew, maintain flexibility in his neck and spine, and execute a quick change of direction and lead when the large circle is reinstated.

Mechanics:
- Ask the horse to lope on the correct lead in the large round circle, at least 50 feet in diameter.
- Visualize a corkscrew pattern with the center of the circle as the eye of the corkscrew.
- Look ahead. Once the horse begins to relax, gradually make smaller and smaller circles, by about five- or ten-foot increments, until you reach the eye.
- Apply even rein pressure back toward your pockets and ask the horse to drop down to a trot.
- At the trot, maintain the forward motion of the front and rear end. This establishes the arc in the horse's spine and creates a similar maneuver as to

Corkscrew exercise: In this skill exercise, begin loping a circle approximately 50 feet in diameter, gradually tightening the circle as you spiral to the center. Drop to a trot in the "eye" of the corkscrew. Hold the horse in four or five circles until he gives his nose and flexes his spine toward the circle. Then trot straight out of the eye, begin loping on the opposite lead, and repeat the exercise from the opposite direction.

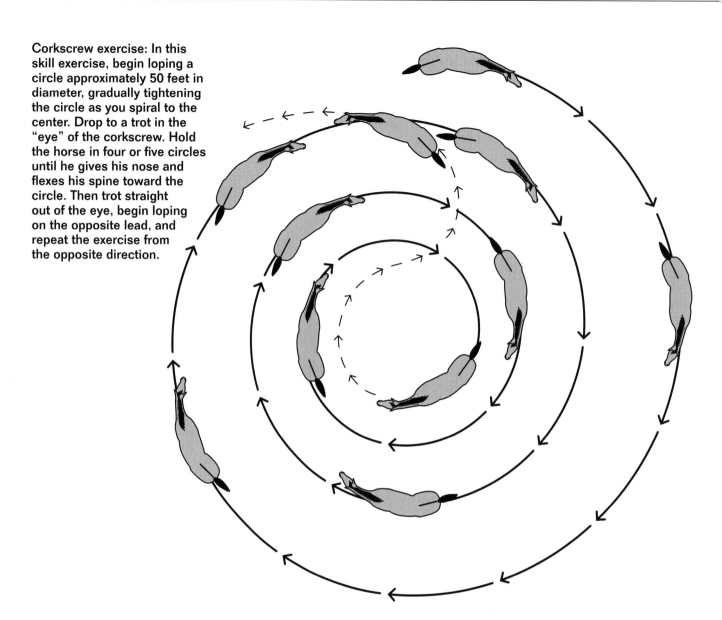

what you would experience in a barrel turn: slight weight in your outside stirrup, body pivoted (inside shoulder back, inside pelvis back), inside hand wide and low, looking about three feet ahead of you into the circle.

- When the horse relaxes and responds with a flexible spine and forward motion, release the rein pressure. Cue him to lope out of the circle in the opposite lead, directly into a large circle to the opposite direction.
- Repeat the exercise in the opposite direction.

Problem 1: You have difficulty establishing the pattern.

Plan:
- Visualize the exercise.
- Plan and ride ahead of yourself. Look about 20 feet ahead.
- Use a lettered or landmarked arena to help you visualize the pattern.
- Remember to gradually decrease the circles in equal increments, shortening your range of vision by five feet each increment.
- Give the horse time to relax and settle into the large circle before starting to spiral.
- Ride both sides of your horse.
- Keep your horse balanced squarely between your hands and legs.
- The horse should not be bent any more

than the degree of bend in the circle.

- Avoid carrying the horse's nose. Too much bend from nose to shoulders causes the horse to step out behind or drop a lead.

Problem 2: Horse cannot stay in a large, even circle and instead drifts out.

Plan:
- Check your position and use of legs, seat, and hands.
- Support your horse in a steady, balanced frame.
- Visualize the size of the large circle.
- Use your outside leg back behind the cinch, and increase the pressure of the outside rein, elevating the outside rein if needed to support the horse.
- Avoid pulling on the inside rein to correct the position, or taking too much outside rein, causing the nose to turn out.
- If resistance is strong, use the inside rein to lead his nose in the direction you wish to go.
- Support this with a strong outside leg. Use your entire leg, from hip to calf. Apply the leg pressure near the horse's back cinch for extra leverage and support.

Problem 3: Horse drifts in and drops his shoulder to inside of the circle.

Plan:
- Check your position and your use of legs, seat, and hands.
- Check to make sure you apply equal pressure on both sides of your horse to support a balanced frame.
- Slightly elevate the inside rein above the neutral position.
- Be ready to apply inside leg pressure or the shoulder/hip correction at the precise moment the horse drifts in.
- Timing is everything. Be fast and accurate. Sometimes an isolated bump to lift and move the rib cage and shoulder back into position is all that is required.

Problem 4: Trouble in the eye of the corkscrew.

Plan:
- Be prepared to correct your horse's body position at every point during the exercise. If he has resistance or difficulty in the big part of the corkscrew, everything will be amplified the smaller the circle becomes.
- Don't try to keep the horse loping in circles too small for his ability or stage of training. Your goal is correct forward movement at any gait. Simply drop to a trot at the point where continuing at a lope would be possible only by sacrificing correct position and forward motion. Precision will come with practice.
- Make sure it is the rider's command for the horse to drop down from a lope to a trot, rather than the horse's idea.

Problem 5: Horse fails to maintain forward motion in the trot phase of the corkscrew, instead pivoting on his front end or hindquarters.

Plan:
- Try squeezing, clucking, or spanking over a hip to reinforce forward motion.
- If the horse's front legs are not moving, kick with both your legs in the front cinch area.

Problem 6: You cannot obtain a slight bend in the horse's spine.

Plan:
- Check your position. Keep your inside hand low and wide to encourage the horse to drop his head.
- Utilize the shoulder/hip correction, if the horse is dropping in. Bumping your heel in the inside flank area instigates more flex; however, overuse of your heel can cause the horse to step out behind.
- Place your free hand on the cantle. This slight shift in weight and posture encourages a light response.

Problem 7: You cannot change directions cleanly and then obtain the correct lead.

Leg yield, arc in straight line: This horse is carrying an arc to the left while traveling in a straight line. My shoulders are parallel with the horse's shoulders.

ward motion instigated from the horse's hind end with energy. Do not stop the horse to obtain a lead change.

Leg Yield

This exercise, in which the horse keeps his body arced while moving forward in a straight line, teaches suppleness. You'll need a fence to help you introduce this skill. Then take the exercise to an open area and "two-track," or move diagonally with the horse's body facing forward and arced.

Application: The basic forward movement developed by this exercise is used in *approaching* a barrel and maintaining a pocket. The exercise encourages the horse to engage his hindquarters for impulsion and to lift his inside shoulder; the leg yield helps support a horse who wants to drop his shoulder or fade into a turn. The exercise also teaches you to use your legs as driving aids to encourage the horse to step up with the inside hind leg. Be careful to not carry the nose in the *approach* to the barrel.

Goal: To create a supple response in the horse's body and increase the use of his inside hock. The exercise helps the horse learn not to drop or fade into the barrel.

Mechanics:
- Rider position in this exercise is very important. *Do not lean.* Your shoulders should be parallel with the horse's shoulders. **Note:** In the accompanying photo, my shoulder is turned slightly to the inside, just as the horse's shoulder is turned to the inside. Increase the pressure of your inside seat bone, to help with the diagonal motion of this exercise.
- Walk with the fence to your side, for example, on your left.
- Take the horse's nose away from the fence (to the right) with a direct rein, and move the horse's front end slightly away from the fence. Keep his hindquarters parallel to the fence with your

Plan:
- Plan ahead for the change. Move from the inside of the corkscrew straight into a large circle in the opposite direction.
- Don't rush. Be definite with cues.
- Maintain impulsion when you change directions and ask for the lope.
- **Note:** If the horse does not obtain the correct lead initially, allow him to lope out three or four strides. Drop down to a trot (simple lead change) and ask again for the correct lead. The most important move to reinforce in the change of direction is impulsion, for-

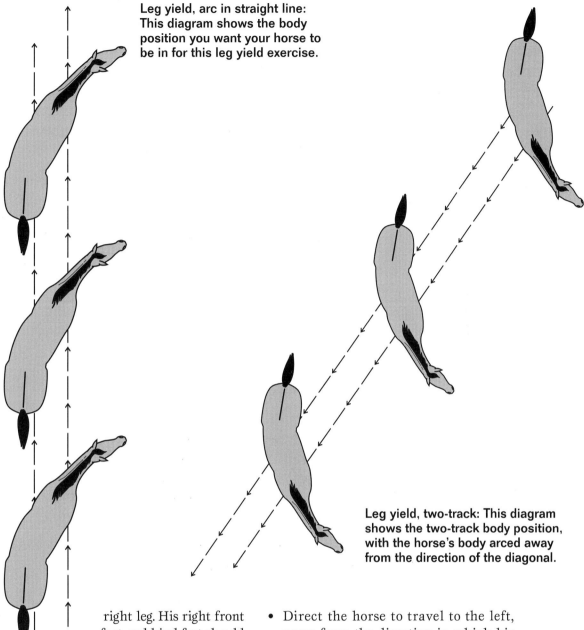

Leg yield, arc in straight line: This diagram shows the body position you want your horse to be in for this leg yield exercise.

Leg yield, two-track: This diagram shows the two-track body position, with the horse's body arced away from the direction of the diagonal.

right leg. His right front foot and hind feet should cross over each other as he moves down the fence.

• Practice at a walk first, then a trot, then a lope.

• When you reach the end of your fence, return to neutral, turn around, and go back down the fence, this time arcing to the left.

• Once you can maintain the arc in a straight line on the fence, try the two-track. Begin by moving forward in a straight line in an open area.

• Ask the horse to arc his body, to the right in this example, just as you did earlier.

• Direct the horse to travel to the left, away from the direction in which his nose is pointed, with your left rein and right foot. Maintain the arc with your right rein.

• At first, practice the leg yield arc for short distances, then gradually increase them.

Problem: Most of this exercise's problems relate to the rider asking the horse for too much arc before having enough forward motion or impulsion. Difficulties for the rider in coordinating rein and leg aids to create the desired response from the horse can also result in a weak execution. When first training, be satisfied with each effort that you and your horse produce, and remember to pat and reward your horse for his effort.

Plan:
- If you're having difficulty with this exercise, remember: impulsion first, then arc.
- Do not pull on both reins. This isolates the forward movement and blocks the horse's ability to create the arc requested.
- Learn to feel the horse's hind leg away from the fence reach up farther than the hind leg on the fence. Remember to create the arc through the horse's whole body, not just in the head and neck.
- Round pen work is a resource in teaching the horse to carry an arc.

Figure-Eight Exercise

This exercise has two circles, approximately 30 feet in diameter, touching to form a common flat side. I use this figure-eight to educate my horses in the formation of direct and indirect arcs. This exercise is a prerequisite to the upcoming "break-off correction."

Application: It creates the forward, balanced motion that is required in the barrel *turn*. It also reinforces the forward reach and push of the inside hock.

Goal: To keep a horse limber from nose through neck and shoulders. Most importantly, it frees up resistance in the horse's back and hindquarters.

Mechanics:
- Start out on a circle at a jog (collected "sitting trot"—slow enough that you don't need to post).
- Use a direct rein to bring and hold the horse's nose toward the inside of the circle. Use little, if any, inside or outside leg pressure. Use outside rein to help support the horse's forward position if necessary.
- Remain in the jog and hold the outside

rein away from the horse. This allows the outside of the horse's body to move over into the area created by opening the outside rein.
- Concentrate on pushing the horse forward with pressure from both legs. Make sure the inside hock is starting to cross up and over the outside hock.
- Complete the circle and go into the straight-line transition of the figure eight. *Do not release the pressure on your horse's nose.*
- Hold your horse's nose through the straight line between the circles, executing a two-track.
- When you begin your circle in the opposite direction, his nose will be to the outside of the circle. For example, if you begin with the horse's nose to the inside on a left circle, his nose will be to the outside when changed to a right circle.
- **Remember:** This is a challenging exercise for the horse to learn. Moving off the rein can be a difficult concept, especially if the concept is not clear to the rider. Reward any effort by the horse to be correct. Don't expect to teach this exercise in one session; it is possibly a three-day process.

Problem: Extreme resistance related to weak areas in the horse's early instruction that involves yielding to pressure.

Plan: Return to the round pen and reestablish the checking exercise. Verify that the horse understands and yields to rein pressure. Verify his willingness to yield to the rein and leg pressure when mounted by checking flexibility, both laterally and vertically.

Shoulder In/ Shoulder Out

In general, this exercise is done at a lope in a large, round circle. For inexperienced riders or horses, it can be introduced at a trot. Using a sequence of cues,

Being able to position your horse any place, any speed, and any time is essential for consistent performance.

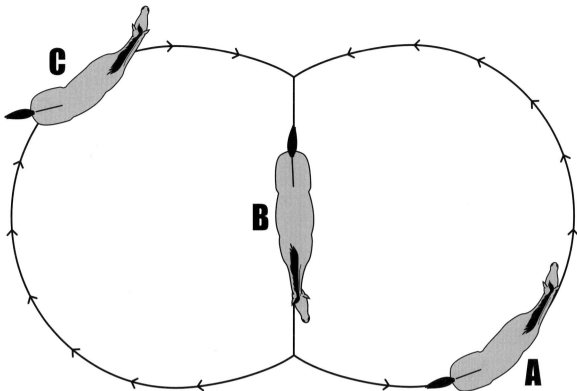

C
B
A

Figure-eight exercise: This exercise deals with direct and indirect arcs. Ride your horse in a circle with his nose to the inside (A). At the intersection of the two circles, ride in a straight line, maintaining your arc and the horse's nose position (B). In the opposite circle, the horse's nose is now to the outside, since he is still traveling on the same arc (C).

the rider can change the position of the horse's shoulders on the circle to help teach framing and balance.

Application: This exercise is the foundation for obtaining the ability to control, balance, and position the horse's body during the *approach* to the barrel. It will provide a tool for dealing with horses who tend to be stiff or who anticipate the turn by dropping their inside shoulders toward a barrel. It will also allow a rider to narrow-up the approach on a horse who tends to drift out.

Goal: To give the horse the ability to respond fluidly and resistance-free to a rider's cues. The horse will have increased maneuverability. He can move his shoulders in or out (left or right) without resistance or lead change. This will allow the rider to obtain consistent position and placement needed in the *approach* and *turn*.

Mechanics—Shoulder to the outside
- Visualize a large circle and begin to

lope in the correct lead. (Remember that this exercise can be introduced at a trot.) Complete six to eight circles, allowing the horse time to relax and focus on the rider.
- Shift your weight onto your outside pelvic bone. Shifting your weight to the outside of the circle helps cue the horse's movement.
- Relax the pressure on the outside rein, to allow room for the horse's shoulder to move out.
- Rotate your inside wrist, turning your hand palm up to reposition the bit in the horse's mouth and request shoulder elevation.
- Elevate your inside hand toward the horse's ear to initiate shoulder elevation. **Note:** Keep each hand on the same side of the neck. Do not cross the hand over the mane. Locate your horse's "sweet spot," the hand position that produces the most responsive result from your horse.
- This sequence of cues is done on a count of four.
- Allow the horse an appropriate time to

respond to the cue. The slower you cue, the quicker the horse will respond.

- Reward the horse's effort by returning his head and shoulder to neutral position on the circle.

Mechanics—Shoulder to the inside

- Visualize a large circle and establish a lope in the correct lead. Complete six to eight circles, allowing the horse time to relax and focus on the rider.
- Shift your weight onto your inside pelvic bone to the inside of the circle.
- Release the inside rein pressure.
- Roll your outside wrist, turning your hand palm up.
- Raise (elevate) your outside hand toward the horse's ear to locate the "sweet spot."
- Hold this for three to five strides and return to neutral position on the circle.

Problem 1: The horse does not maintain his lead during the exercise. This may indicate the horse is not supple in the spine or is not giving to rein pressure.

Plan:
- Return to the normal, relaxed position on the circle.
- Drop to a trot.
- Reinstate the correct lead.
- Recue for the exercise.

Problem 2: You fail to make a definite shift in weight before using the rein aid.

Plan: Remember your four-count sequence. Always start by shifting your weight, and allow a stride or two before instituting the second cue.

Problem 3: You hurry the sequence of cues, not allowing the horse time to settle and respond.

Plan:
- Pay attention and make sure the horse has adequate time to respond to each cue.
- Focus on the sequence and allow two to three seconds between each cue.

- Be clear in your cues. Do not send mixed signals. Make sure you understand the exercise.

Problem 4: You request too many strides at one time, and fail to reward the effort and response from the horse.

Plan:
- Remember to reward the slightest effort, two to three strides, especially in early training.

Problem 5: You fail to elevate your hand up the horse's neck toward the ear to counteract resistance. Reining back towards your chest creates resistance.

Plan: Remember to find the hand position that produces the correct response with the least amount of effort for each horse, the sweet spot. **Note:** Do not cross your hand over the neck. The farther up the neck and higher your hand position, the greater the leverage. Do not rein back toward your chest, belt, or pocket. Lift your rein toward the horse's ear.

Problem 6: Your horse resists the exercise by losing his forward motion.

Plan:
- Make sure you are asking for forward motion with your legs, reinforcing with a verbal cue, a cluck, and a spank if needed.
- Make sure you elevate your hand, reinforcing forward motion with the outside rein if necessary.

Problem 7: You can't seem to coordinate your legs, hand, and seat in order to correct a horse who may object strongly to taking the shoulder to the inside. In extreme situations, the horse "stampedes," or rushes away from the pressure in a panicked fashion.

Plan:
- Prevention is the best answer. Ensure that the horse understands the figure-

Proficiency in the skill exercises will help you identify your horse's strong and weak areas as you progress to the barrel pattern.

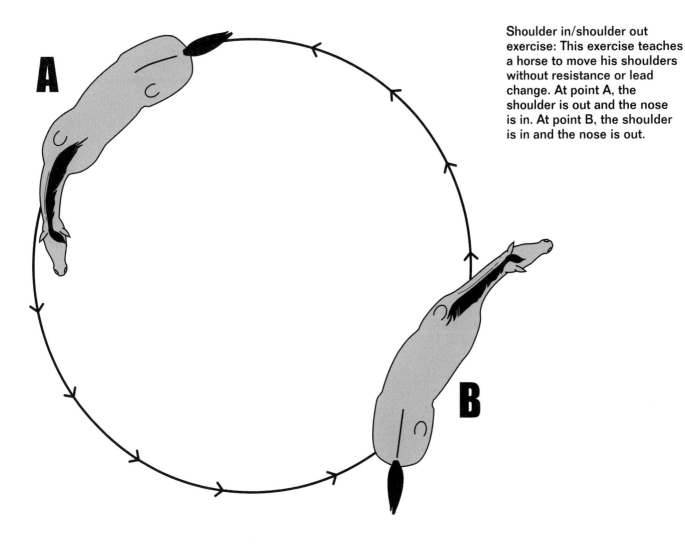

A

B

Shoulder in/shoulder out exercise: This exercise teaches a horse to move his shoulders without resistance or lead change. At point A, the shoulder is out and the nose is in. At point B, the shoulder is in and the nose is out.

Shoulder in/shoulder out exercise: Find the "sweet spot," the exact hand position that produces your horse's best response to your rein aid. Here, I have rolled my wrist, palm up, to elevate the horse's shoulder. Raise your hand toward the horse's ear for increased leverage for elevation.

Rating: This exercise teaches the horse to shorten or lengthen his stride at your request. First, roll your pelvis under and sit heavy on your back pockets (1). Then rein back toward your pockets with steady pressure (2). Hold that pressure until the horse shortens his stride (3), then release.

eight exercise before attempting the shoulder-in/shoulder-out exercise.

- If possible, use a large round pen with good footing the first time you ask the horse to complete this exercise. This helps the horse and rider to stay focused as they work through any resistance.
- Introduce this exercise at a trot to slow the reaction time and reinforce cues. **Note:** Extreme reactions are generally caused by inadequate foun-

dation, a confused horse and rider, or the rider's difficulty in using the proper sequence of the aids.

- Reward any effort by the horse to complete the exercise.

Rating

Many of the errors in overrun barrels and poorly executed turns are related to a failure to obtain *rate*. I use an exercise called rating to reinforce a horse's ability to rate on command from the rider. In the exercise, the horse lengthens and shortens his stride at the specific moment requested by the rider.

Application: Being able to rate your horse at any place, any time, and any speed ensures a balanced, accurate, and precise collection and rate during your barrel run.

Goal: To allow your horse to respond to a shift in your weight by shortening or lengthening his stride. In time, he will respond to your cue on the barrel course by shortening his stride as you move into the *turn* and lengthening his stride in between the *turns*.

Mechanics—Lengthen strides:
- Strides should be as long as possible.
- The hindquarters need to produce impulsion.
- The horse needs to remain calm, balanced, and light on the forehand.
- The horse needs to remain in contact with the bit, with his head and neck lowered and lengthened, so that his strides become longer, rather than higher. Take caution not to overtuck the horse's nose.
- The horse should not speed up so that his strides become hurried.
- Don't misinterpret: *Impulsion* is not the same as speed.

Mechanics—Rating:
- Lope or trot a large circle, using the correct lead or diagonal.
- Establish a steady speed. Pick a "pretend speed" for your own reference—15, 20, or 25 mph, etc.
- Once the horse is relaxed and balanced, roll your pelvis, squeeze your legs to maintain impulsion, and sit heavy on your back pockets.
- Pause and hold.
- Rein back to your pockets with increased pressure until the horse shortens his stride, slowing from an imaginary 20 mph to 10 mph, or from a long trot to a jog.
- Once the horse collects and maintains this slower speed, reward him by releasing the increased rein pressure and allow the horse to increase his momentum back to the original speed.

Problem: Horse stiffens in response to cue, his weight stays heavy on forehand, or he does not shorten stride or slow gait.

Plan: Seesaw the reins lightly to supple horse's poll and jaw; work to regain his attention. Hold the reins firm until the horse backs off and responds to command. Maintain your supple, relaxed body posture; avoid becoming rigid in legs and thighs. **Remember:** Tighten hands to apply pressure, open hands to release pressure.

Backing

The horse must have good impulsion forward before he can have a good reverse.

Application: Establishing a correct reverse on a horse gives the rider a tool to reinforce *rate* and establish the horse's willingness to yield through his entire body to rein pressure.

Goal: To teach a horse to shift his weight off his forehand, thereby collecting and efficiently using his hindquarters.

Mechanics:
- Visualize walking, not dragging, your horse in reverse.
- Create some energy with your legs and reins, as if you were going to ask the horse to walk forward by using your seat and legs.
- At the very moment the horse feels like he is going to take a forward step, pick up the reins and hold with light rein pressure to ask for the reverse. Simulate the feeling of marching in the saddle by lifting left and right side of pelvis. This allows the horse to lift his back

Backing: Create energy as if you're asking your horse to walk forward. When you think he's about to step forward, pick up the reins and ask him to back with steady rein pressure and by squeezing with your legs behind the cinch to create impulsion.

and at the same time step backwards.

- If the horse gets heavy and drags, he has lost his impulsion and is not utilizing his body. Activate his steps by squeezing or bumping your legs behind the cinch to increase impulsion from the rear or squeeze or bump by the front cinch or shoulders to lighten up the front, depending on which direction the resistance is coming from.
- Build on the length of the reverse three to five steps at a time.
- **Note:** Don't lose patience. Don't get mad. Never jerk. In most cases an unresponsive horse doesn't understand the rider's commands or does not understand the concepts of impulsion.

Problem: Horse resists responding to your rein or leg cues, possibly bracing on your hand, tossing or throwing his head, opening his mouth, rearing, or refusing to take a step backwards.

Plan:
- Make sure your horse is not sore. For instance, sore backs, sore mouths, sore stifles, and sore hocks can produce resistance.
- Make sure that your equipment is adjusted correctly.
- If the problem is extreme resistance (rearing, freezing up, and/or lunging forward) and not physical or mechanical, the horse needs his foundation reinforced. Return to the exercises on and off the horse that establish his response of yielding to rein pressure.
- If the resistance seems related to an attitude, the double-down correction can be used to refocus the horse. Refer to Chapter 6.
- Make sure you are creating impulsion by using your legs. Impulsion is movement forward or in reverse with energy and should not be confused with speed.
- Sometimes a light one-two see-saw on the reins aids in regaining a horse's attention and lightens up his response.
- **Note:** You may need to seek assistance from a qualified trainer to help you work through cases of extreme resistance.

Stopping at the Fence

There are several exercises that benefit from using the arena fence as a training tool. The arena fence can be most productive in training stops and rollbacks.

Application: Developing the ability of the horse to *rate* has a direct impact on the quality and quickness of the horse's *turn*. The stop and rollback exercises help develop the horse's physical and mental responsiveness, enabling the rider to be effective regardless of the speed.

Goal: To create a horse who can shorten his stride on command and remain physi-

Stopping at the fence: Approximately five strides before the fence, sit down. Pause, then say whoa and pick up on the reins to remove slack but do not pull. Let the fence reinforce the stop by preventing forward motion.

cally balanced in order to use his body to produce a quick, tight *turn*.

Mechanics:
- Trot or lope in a large circle at the end of an arena or fenced riding area with two corners.
- When the horse relaxes, lope up the fence toward one of the corners.
- Approximately five strides before the corner, ask for the stop using this sequence:
- Sit down in the saddle (roll your pelvis by pulling your bellybutton back and rounding your spine).
- Say whoa.
- Pick up on the reins and bring your hands back toward your pockets. Hold for the stop, but do not pull.
- If the horse doesn't respond, let the fence reinforce the stop by preventing forward motion.
- If the horse responds to the rider's command, the rider then has three choices: back two or three steps and quit, instigate a 360-degree pivot, or roll back in

opposite direction to reinforce horse's weight shift off the front end and help teach precision.

Problem: Horse refuses to balance weight off front end and bounces through the stop.

Plan: Back the horse a few steps through the stop to reinforce the weight shift off the front end. Then, roll back to outside of circle and re-execute the exercise. Two to three stops in a session is usually enough. The rider should plan six weeks to three months to train a proper and balanced stop before moving off the fence with the exercise.

Stopping With an Arc

This exercise involves maintaining an arc in the horse's spine while executing a stop. It is more complex than a regular stop and should not be done until the horse can maintain a straight and supple body position in a regular stop. Like all

Rollback: Back until the horse shifts his weight onto his hindquarters (1). With the inside (right) rein, take the horse's nose to the two o'clock position (2). Release inside rein, pick up outside (left) rein, and use outside leg to send the horse's body around after his nose (3). Elevate your outside hand and lower your inside hand, if needed (4). Send your horse in the opposite direction with energy (5).

exercises beginning at the trot, this will help horse and rider understand the mechanics of the maneuver.

Application: This exercise teaches the horse to move his inside hock up and forward to facilitate a turn or rollback position.

Goal: To teach the horse the position that will help him *rate* and *turn* his barrels.

Mechanics:

- Use a little inside rein and outside leg pressure to establish the arc, with nose and hip toward the fence.
- After the arc is set, ask for the stop.
- Sit down.
- Say whoa.
- Pick up on the reins. Follow through with outside rein pressure to limit forward movement and help maintain body position.
- The horse's inside hock moves up and forward into turn or rollback position.
- Two-track helps prepare a horse for this advanced theory.
- Once the horse begins stopping with

the fence as an aid, ask for a stop halfway down the fence or in a circle. This exercise establishes the horse's confidence that he can stop in the open. If the stop falters, return to the reinforcement of the fence.

Rollback

This exercise involves a direction change and requires the horse to shift his weight to his hindquarters and pivot off his inside hock.

Application: The rollback exercise teaches the horse how to collect himself in order to shorten his stride and drive away from a barrel.

Goal: To produce a horse who will be responsive when the rider picks up the reins. The horse will be looking for ground to get into or someplace to go. The exercise will help the horse stay balanced for an efficient turn, and push off his hocks when he changes direction or leaves the turn.

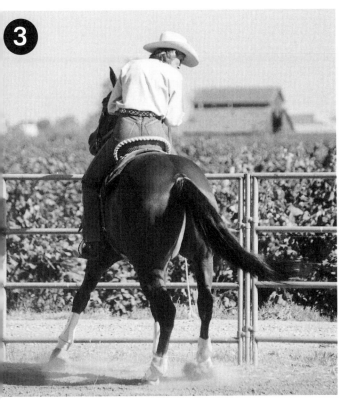

Mechanics:

- Travel parallel along a fence and cue for a stop.
- To assist with positioning, visualize the face of a clock with 12:00 straight ahead. For a rollback to the right, visualize the 2:00 position. For a rollback to the left, visualize the 10:00 position.
- Back until the horse shifts his weight onto his hindquarters.
- Using a direct rein to initiate the direction of the rollback, take the horse's nose toward the fence to the two o'clock position or the ten o'clock position.
- As the horse starts the turn, release some of the nose pressure and lay the outside rein and outside leg simultaneously against the horse to push his body in the direction of his nose in order to roll off his hocks out of the rollback.
- Make sure the horse uses his inside hock to push off in a forward motion. This maneuver is not just a stop and pivot.
- **Note:** The horse's weight has already been shifted toward the hindquarters from the stop. The fence will act as an

aid to keep his weight distributed on his hindquarters. This will help him to pivot on his inside hind leg. With any skill exercise, the horse must be shown the execution at a slow and precise rate of speed. Dropping to a trot helps build confidence in the horse and rider. The skill can be worked at a variety of speeds, even out of a large circle for advanced horses and riders.

- After the rollback has been completed, help the horse remain calm if he becomes hyper or nervous. Circle until his mind settles before taking him out of the circle and back up the opposite fence. It is important to make the rollback a smooth, continuous motion, without hesitation, as the horse sets, turns, and leaves in the opposite direction. When the stop and rollback exercise is introduced, the focus is not necessarily on the correct lead, but more on movement and impulsion. With practice, the horse should break out of the rollback in the correct lead toward the next circle.

Problem: As the horse begins to respond to cues, he may begin to anticipate the stop.

Plan: Use your legs to push the horse into the stop position. When he stops nicely and gets into the ground, reward him with a pat, before calling it a day or progressing to the next exercise.

Note: Caution should be taken to not overdo this exercise. Though the individual horse will dictate the amount of pressure he can handle, three to five rollbacks is usually enough for one session.

As the horse advances from dependencies on aids, progress to rollbacks out of a circle. Lope circles in the arena. Sit and cue with the outside rein, without bringing the horse to a complete stop. Roll back to the outside of the circle and reverse direction, picking up the opposite lead. If you feel that the horse needs the reinforcement of the fence, move the circle closer to a side fence. The fence can be once

Ninety percent of a horse's riding time should be spent outside the arena.

again used to reinforce rate, before returning to a rollback in the open.

45-Degree Angle Into the Fence and Stop

Another way to use the fence to teach the stop is to move the circle closer to the side of the arena, approaching the fence at a 45-degree angle. The rider's ability to visualize and ride the horse into a 45-degree approach is key to the success of this exercise. It is helpful to use the lettered or landmarked arena system to help the rider structure the exercise.

Refer to the application and goals of using the fence as a training aid.

Mechanics:
- Trot or lope a large circle.
- Identify a letter or landmark on the fence as a place to aim your 45-degree approach and stop into the fence.
- Keep your horse between your hands and legs, balanced and straight. Maintain a 45-degree angle as you ride to your letter or point.
- As you approach the letter with your straight horse, on a 45-degree angle to the wall, plan for your stop.
- Sit first, then say whoa. Pick up the reins and hold gently back toward your pockets until the horse stops. Use your legs to squeeze impulsion if he is not shifting his weight off the forehand.
- **Note:** This is the point where the wall reinforces and helps the horse to stop, without the rider having to pull hard on the reins or fight the horse. The rider allows the horse to make the choice to stop, and the fence restricts the movement.
- Back up the horse if he bounces on the forehand or pushes through the stop. This distributes the horse's weight away from the front end.
- Reverse or roll the horse back into the opposite circle if additional circles and stops are required.

Problem 1: You fail to ride to the fence in a 45-degree angle.

Plan:
- Visualize your approach.
- Use a visual cue to help you aim your horse to the correct spot.
- Ride ahead of yourself.
- Use both legs to help maintain forward impulsion.

Problem 2: Your horse does not stay straight in the approach to the fence.

Plan:
- Maintain light contact (a feel) with your horse's mouth.
- Use leg and rein aids to keep the horse moving straight. This frames and balances the horse's shoulder and rib cage.

Problem 3: You cue with the rein before sitting or saying whoa.

Plan:
- Verbalize the sequence out loud.
- Sit and say whoa first to prepare the horse for the stop; then cue with the rein.
- Allow the horse time to respond.

Problem 4: You have trouble with timing your cues. As a result, your horse props, braces, tosses his head, or hits the fence.

Plan:
- Get assistance, if indicated, from a qualified ground person to help you identify your weak areas.
- Increase your knowledge of good horsemanship. Al Dunning's *Western Horseman* book *Reining Completely Revised* is a wonderful reference. (To order, visit www.westernhorseman.com.)
- Be sure to allow time for the horse to respond to each cue.
- Be smooth with your cues.

Problem 5: You repeat the exercise too often, and your horse begins to anticipate the stop before you cue him, or becomes high-strung or agitated.

Plan:
- Do not overdo the exercise. Three to five stop attempts are enough for one training session.
- Remember to return to large, neutral circles until the horse relaxes before asking for the stop.
- Remember to reward the horse's efforts to correctly respond to the rider's request.
- Mix this exercise with the corkscrew, all rights or all lefts exercises, or circles to help prevent the horse from getting high.

Conclusion

Each of these exercises can blend from one to another. The rider can choreograph a rhythmic dance that incorporates skills to reinforce the strengths and weaknesses in the horse's training and foundation.

By creating a no-stop/no-start approach to these skill-building exercises, the horse will not anticipate and or become anxious about what is coming next. Unless the rider is rewarding a horse for a particularly nice move, do not stop motion after one exercise is completed. Be creative; go from one exercise to another as the horse's strengths and weaknesses dictate.

Caution should be taken to not over-drill or fatigue the horse during a training session. Knowing when to quit is an important aspect of successful training. A horse's attention span is much shorter than a human's; the average is possibly as short as eight to fifteen minutes.

Vary the pressure and the difficulty of the skill exercise depending on the individual's ability to stay responsive and focused on the rider. Most likely, if a horse gets too tired, the session will end in frustration for both horse and rider. Use horse or rider mistakes as additional opportunities to train, and reward the horse's efforts to please the rider.

Remember that there will always be another day and another opportunity to train. A good rule of thumb: 90 percent of a horse's riding time should be spent outside the arena.

5

NOW FOR THE BARRELS

A good foundation in barrel racing basics allows a horse to develop an individual style based on his individual abilities.

YOUR HORSE'S ability to successfully complete the skill-building exercises covered in Chapter 4 indicates that he is ready to begin work on the barrel pattern. The skill exercises help create a horse who is responsive to direct and indirect rein and leg pressure, can pick up both leads, and will rate and stop on command.

All of these responses give your horse the ability to be guided and positioned. This basic foundation will provide the tools necessary to introduce the horse to the A.R.T.

Using the cone system helps you visualize the proper paths around the barrels and the positioning for your horse for approaching, rating, and turning each barrel.

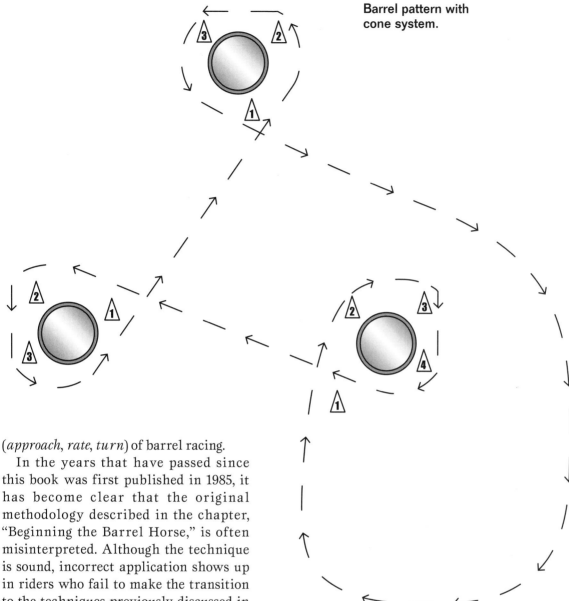

Barrel pattern with cone system.

(*approach*, *rate*, *turn*) of barrel racing.

In the years that have passed since this book was first published in 1985, it has become clear that the original methodology described in the chapter, "Beginning the Barrel Horse," is often misinterpreted. Although the technique is sound, incorrect application shows up in riders who fail to make the transition to the techniques previously discussed in "Advanced Barrel Work."

Starting a young horse by approaching a barrel straight begins to teach a horse to arc into turning position. However, after the horse learns to move off leg pressure, continuing the practice of going straight to the barrel and then moving over into the pocket point creates a tendency for riders to carry too much nose. This movement tends to encourage horses to make too wide of a pocket, allowing them to escape through their shoulders in the turn. Dropped leads may also result.

To help riders avoid this problem, this book defines the barrel pattern by the ele-

ments of approach, rate, and turn and redirects the horse's approach directly to the pocket point.

Cone System

As a training and teaching device, the cone system helps you visualize the pattern in elements of the approach, rate, and turn at each barrel. Each cone will remind you of the precise place where you need to cue your horse for a specific response.

The first cone is the first point at which

Cone system, first barrel: The rate point can be adjusted according to the individual horse's level of training and athletic ability. This horse is being rated at the first cone.

Cone system, first barrel: The additional cone (2) on the first barrel helps the rider teach the horse to maintain his pocket as he begins the barrel turn.

The no stop/no start method helps keep a horse from becoming agitated or anticipating repetitious work.

you can ask your horse to rate. Depending on your horse's experience, maturity, and athletic ability, your rate point can be anywhere between the first and second cone position.

An additional cone at the first barrel, numbered 2 in the photos of the first barrel, will help you and your horse maintain his pocket as he moves up into the turn.

The second cone (cone 3 in the first-barrel photos) provides the second option for the rate point. It is also the place to start the turn. Pick up your inside rein and shift your weight to your outside stirrup. Then look and drive your horse to the last cone.

The last cone indicates where to place the horse to finish the turn. If necessary, use outside rein to direct your horse's body to finish the turn close to the barrel. This final position enables your horse to leave

in a forward full stride, with his chest and hip aimed straight to the pocket point for the next barrel.

No Stop/No Start

In addition to the cone placement, the use of the no stop/no start method is critical in keeping the horse from becoming agitated and anticipating the repetitious work necessary to pattern the barrel horse.

After completing the turn around the third barrel, angle your horse toward the fence on the same side of the arena as your first barrel. Travel down the side fence until you're even with your starting point for the pattern. Then curve around and move back into the pattern, with no stops and no starts.

Cone system, first barrel: The rider looks and drives the horse to the last cone position. This gives the horse room to finish the turn so his movement to the second barrel approach is straight.

Left: Cone system, first barrel: The third cone on the first barrel reminds the rider to maintain pocket position through the turn. The rider picks up the inside rein for direction followed by the outside rein to help balance the horse's shoulder position. Shifting weight slightly to the outside stirrup helps create a fast, fluid turn.

Cone system, first barrel: At the last cone, the rider uses the outside rein to direct the horse's body to follow his nose and finish the turn close to the barrel, which directly aims him into the approach position for the second barrel.

Cone system, leaving the first barrel: The path away from the first barrel passes between the last cone and cone one. Cone one helps the horse stay straight as he aims into the second barrel approach.

Cone system, second barrel: The rider looks and rides to the pocket point for the second barrel. The horse can be rated at the first cone or between the first and second cones depending on the horse's ability to shorten his stride and prepare for the turn. Because the second barrel is usually closer to a fence, the rate position should be closer to the desired turn.

Cone system, second barrel: At the second cone, the rider takes the horse's nose, cueing him to start the turn.

Regardless of the size of the pocket or the stage of training, the horse must finish his turn close to the barrel in order to be in alignment for his next approach, rate, and turn position.

Starting the Pattern

In the beginning start by working the horse at a jog. Remember to allow for enough pocket coming into the barrel. The pocket is the amount of room the rider gives the horse to obtain a well-positioned and fluid turn.

The size of the pocket is adjusted to the training level of the horse. A larger pocket provides every opportunity for the beginning barrel horse to be correct and confident in his turn. As the horse progresses in his training, the size of the pocket can be reduced.

Regardless of the pocket size or stage of training, the horse must finish his turn close to the barrel. Pattern work and attention to cone position is most important in the early stages of training.

At first, rate is not important because you are already traveling slow. However, when riding to the first cone position, practice the rider position for rate: Roll your pelvis under, almost as if you're attempting to sit on your back pockets. This will help introduce the horse to the fact he will be taught to shorten his stride at this point.

At the second cone, start the turn by shifting your weight to the outside stirrup and picking up on the inside rein. This cues the horse for the turn. If necessary, achieve impulsion by applying pressure with both legs at the front cinch area.

Now look and aim the horse to the third or last cone position. Using the outside rein cues the horse's body to follow his nose and aids in a tight, finished turn. At this time the horse should be aimed in position to approach the next pocket point. This position creates an early approach and prepares the rider for the second barrel turn.

Begin the sequence again at the second barrel. Ride the horse to the pocket point; request rate at or between the first or second cone. Pick up on the inside rein and start the horse's turn. Ride to the third or last cone. At the last cone again use the outside rein, if necessary, to help the horse finish the turn.

The third barrel has the same sequence: approach, rate, and turn. The only change

Cone system, second barrel: The rider looks and aims for the third cone. The horse is moving through the turn and maintaining a slight arc in his spine.

Cone system, second barrel: At the third cone, the rider uses the outside rein, if necessary, to cue the horse to finish the turn with his body aimed straight into the third barrel approach and pocket.

is the 360-degree turn around the third barrel and the angle down the fence to initiate the return to the first barrel into the no stop/no start pattern.

A balanced horse and rider are critical. Be prepared to frame the horse around all the turns and in between the barrels. Using two reins will help the rider accomplish this position.

As a rule of thumb, start a green horse by jogging through the barrel pattern approximately eight to ten times a day, three to five days a week. The pattern during the early stages can be varied. For example,

Cone system, third barrel: Correct finish on the second barrel gives you proper placement in the approach to the third barrel. The horse maintains a balanced position as he is cued for the rate at cones one or two, depending on the horse.

Cone system, third barrel: At the second cone, the rider picks up the inside rein and shifts her weight to the outside stirrup to cue the horse to start the turn.

complete the pattern, going around all three barrels. Then go around just the first and third barrels before returning to the no stop/no start program. The focus at this point is to teach response and position in a turn, not the cloverleaf pattern.

The all right/all left exercise is a great exercise to start a green horse loping the barrel pattern. Refer to the diagrams in this chapter for the mechanics of the exercise. Remember not to tighten any circle more than the horse's ability to maintain

Cone system, third barrel: The rider looks and rides to the third cone position. The horse maintains balanced, correct body alignment. The rider may have to create impulsion through the turn with leg pressure to help drive the horse forward.

Cone system, third barrel: If necessary, the rider uses the outside rein to help the horse's body finish the turn. The rider plans to finish the third barrel by riding at an angle to the side fence. She can then travel down the fence, circle back, and restart the pattern without stopping (no stop/no start). This avoids apprehension of the horse at stopping and starting the pattern.

When asking for rate, the angle of your hips changes from this …

… to this. Your back rounds and your pelvis rolls under, almost as if you're trying to sit on your back pockets.

The quality of your training sessions will help create confidence both for you and for your horse.

the lope. For example, a green horse could be taken from a 40-foot circle to a 20-foot circle and returned to a 40-foot circle. A more advanced horse can be asked for a tighter circle. Remember to reward the horse's effort in the small circle by returning to a larger, neutral circle. Creating the element of confidence is important in training.

Do not overwork the barrel pattern. The horse can get tired, bored, and soured. Once that happens, a horse's attitude is hard to readjust. Be a creative trainer. Make the education fun.

The barrels are just a visual aid to which the horse should respond. Some days our focus is conditioning; other days the focus can be in the arena on skill-building exercises. Ninety percent of our riding should be outside the arena. Remember that the barrels are not like cattle and offer little incentive for the horse to enjoy his work. The pattern and arena work can be mundane and boring. Be creative; for example, follow a conditioning session with light pattern work. Remember to allow the horse's weak areas to dictate the exercises you will work on.

Rating

After the initial introduction to the barrel pattern, begin to introduce rate, which on the barrel pattern is the horse's ability to shorten his stride and prepare for placement in the turn. Practice cueing for rate with consistent cues and rewards, important elements in teaching a horse to rate a barrel consistently regardless of speed.

To introduce rate on the barrel pattern, approach the barrel pocket at a jog with the horse's shoulder, rib cage, and hips framed and balanced between the reins. Use the first cone as a visual cue to position and ask for rate. Sit, say "whoa," and pick up on the reins.

As you feel the horse shorten his stride, you may need to apply leg pressure to drive the hindquarters up under the horse, to help shorten his stride, and to drive him forward through the turn. Allow the horse to shorten his stride and continue jogging through the turn. Once the turn is completed, jog the horse to the next pocket and again ask for rate by going through the same sequence.

Your rate point can be adjusted to any

Rating: Rider body position and the sequence of cues for rate do not vary from barrel to barrel (although the rate point might vary with each horse or with the arena conditions). To introduce the rate sequence, approach the barrel at a jog.

Rating: Sit, say "whoa," and gently increase rein pressure back toward your pockets.

place between the first and second cones, depending on the individual horse's needs and ability to respond to the rider's cues. This position will vary between horses and can be adjusted as training advances and the horse becomes more responsive.

Rate is reinforced in two ways. When the horse feels the rider sit deep on his back, because of his preliminary training, he responds by shortening his stride. This initial cue decreases the amount of reinforcement the rider gives with the reins. The horse learns that when he is working barrels, "whoa" doesn't mean stop, it means rate—shorten the stride and prepare to turn. If you want the horse to come to a complete stop, take a little firmer hold with the reins and apply less leg pressure.

To continue to reinforce the mechanics of rating on a green horse, drop down a gait before setting up the turn (from a jog to a walk, from a lope to a trot). Later, as training advances, you can begin to simply shorten the stride from a gallop to a lope. The momentum of the approach will

Rating: The horse should respond by shifting his weight to his hindquarters and shortening his stride.

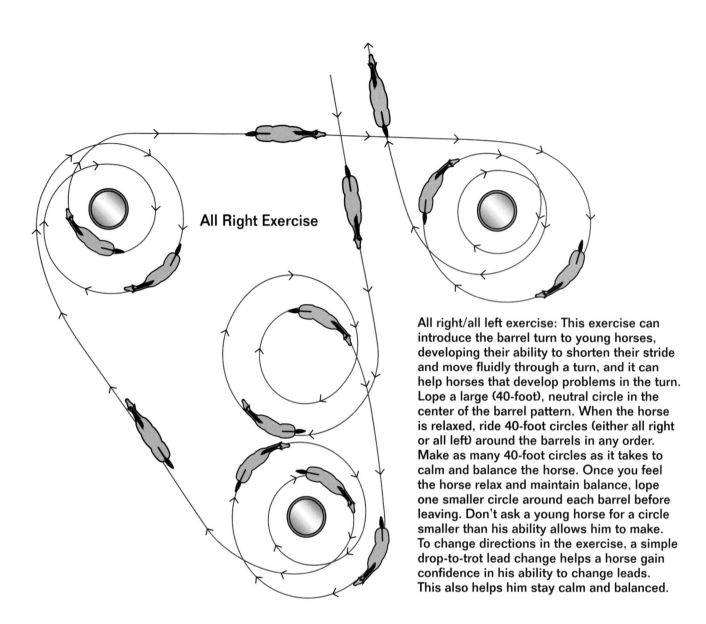

All Right Exercise

All right/all left exercise: This exercise can introduce the barrel turn to young horses, developing their ability to shorten their stride and move fluidly through a turn, and it can help horses that develop problems in the turn. Lope a large (40-foot), neutral circle in the center of the barrel pattern. When the horse is relaxed, ride 40-foot circles (either all right or all left) around the barrels in any order. Make as many 40-foot circles as it takes to calm and balance the horse. Once you feel the horse relax and maintain balance, lope one smaller circle around each barrel before leaving. Don't ask a young horse for a circle smaller than his ability allows him to make. To change directions in the exercise, a simple drop-to-trot lead change helps a horse gain confidence in his ability to change leads. This also helps him stay calm and balanced.

carry a horse through his turn. Eventually it's the momentum, impulsion, and proper positioning that will "slingshot" the horse around a barrel and provide a well-timed and efficient turn.

Observations

Often riders approach a barrel, then ask the horse to speed up for the turn. They might believe this aids in creating a quicker turn. However, it seems to make most horses high and silly as they approach a barrel and anticipate this command. Remember that forward impulsion is important to moving a horse through his

turn. Effective impulsion is created by the rider's effective use of hand and leg cues.

Snap and quickness in turns are certainly important, but effective turns are built with precise and proper body position and consistent cues. Backing off pressure in the turns allows the horse time to gather and balance himself through the turn. Properly planned turns help him push off and make a fast turn. This philosophy encourages the horse to gain confidence in his job, instead of becoming apprehensive of the barrel pattern.

It is important to realize that the faster a horse is traveling, the more critical your precise request for rate. Where you ask for rate will depend on your

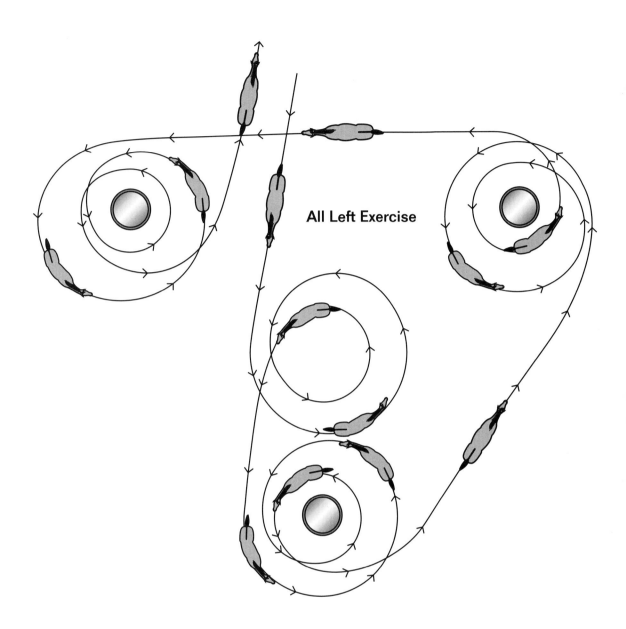

All Left Exercise

horse's ability to respond.

Chapter 6, "Problem Solving," addresses one of the main problems a barrel horse can develop: "slicing" a barrel. One way a horse learns to slice is by the rider asking him to rate too early, usually because the rider isn't sure how to adjust the horse's first cone rate position as the horse advances in his training. As the rider slows him down to make a turn, the horse can anticipate his turn by dropping or fading into the barrel with his shoulder.

With the correct foundation, learned in the stop and rollback exercises, a horse can be requested—any place, any speed, any time—to rate. When the rider sits and picks up the reins, the horse should respond to the command. This builds the rider's ability to run fast and confidently in the approach to each barrel. Deviations from the horse's responsiveness can be corrected by returning to the exercises developed to reinforce rate.

Getting Faster

When the horse is jogging and loping consistently through the barrel pattern, sneak in a faster run every few training sessions. Use the no stop/no start routine. Be sure to jog through the course until the horse's mind settles, but don't jog so long it makes him bored or reduces his

This series of photos demonstrates a first barrel turn at a lope without the use of cones. The rider is using both reins to help the horse maintain his position. Proper *approach* and *rate* mean the horse is balanced and has been taught to collect for the *turn*.

The rider uses the inside rein to start the turn, ...

On the practice pattern, make corrections at any time or speed if the horse or rider is not correct.

incentive. After jogging around the third barrel, request a lope in the correct lead for the first barrel as you travel down the fence to once again start the pattern.

When the horse begins to pay attention, pick up some speed going toward the first barrel and allow him to gallop through the course. Make corrections if and when necessary at any time or place on the pattern.

Take note: Make corrections at any time or speed during training when either the horse or rider is not correct. The rider has approximately five seconds to correct a move before the horse registers it as correct. Make sure the bit affords the control you need as speed increases, and make sure the horse not only accepts the bridle choice but is confident in its control. Consistent reward and discipline help create consistency in training and competition. The horse needs to know what the rider is asking.

Most importantly, the rider needs to know what she or he is asking of the horse. Some riders change according to which "trainer" they talked to the previous evening. Imagine the frustration of the

horse when he is cued inconsistently and then is suddenly disciplined for what he has been allowed to get away with in the past.

It is important for the rider to stay relaxed when speed is increased. The horse is a mirror image of the rider's emotions and training ability. Most important, as speed increases, remain consistent to your training philosophy and ride your horse between your hands while looking and riding straight to your chosen pocket position. Rate, and then feel the horse shorten his stride before asking for the turn. This makes it easier for him to stay balanced and hold his leads with speed. The position builds a productive, well-planned turn.

Seasoning

When the horse becomes solid on barrels at a variety of speeds at home, it's time to make some runs away from his home arena. A couple of times a week haul to a neighbor's house or a jackpot, to practice time-only runs. Many times a young horse

... rides to the last cone position, and ...

...if necessary, uses the outside rein to direct the horse's body to complete the turn.

As they leave the barrel, their position will create the correct *approach* to the second barrel's pocket point. Notice the horse's chest and hindquarters are aligned in straight position to the next pocket point.

will feel solid in his own arena, but in a new arena he becomes insecure in his surroundings. Sometimes this is caused by the rider's insecurity or lack of confidence. This type of local hauling is the first step in seasoning a young or green horse and helps create a more seasoned rider.

This can be a volatile time for a barrel horse. When you take him away from his environment, he is under stress from hauling and new noises associated with the road and competitions. Give him a little extra consideration. Don't pressure him too much on a new pattern. If he does not respond the way he should, be patient. Be productive in the session even if you just go back to the reinforcement of the basic skill exercises before putting him away.

Hint: Hauling a young horse, who might be somewhat insecure, with an older, solid,

Getting faster: The *approach*, *rate*, and *turn* remain consistent when speed is applied. The rider cues for rate by sitting deep in the saddle at the proper cone position for the horse before taking the slack out of the reins (here, the second cone position).

The time it takes to make a barrel horse depends on the attitude and ability of both horse and rider.

and emotionally stable horse will help settle the inexperienced horse and reinforce positive reactions and responses.

The period of time it takes to make a barrel horse varies. I believe it takes approximately one to three years from start to finish. This time frame depends upon the horse's attitude and his initial foundation of training, and the ability and knowledge of the rider. Consideration should be taken in identifying the type of competition planned for the horse.

It took four years between rodeo schedules to train my old horse Seven. Once I started hauling him, he didn't need much seasoning. He started winning right away. So, are you going to put in more time in your own arena and shorten the seasoning period? Or will you cheat on the time spent at home and spend more time on the road? I believe in training at home and competing when I leave. For one thing, it's a lot more economical.

Final Thought

At my clinics students learn traditional horsemanship skills that apply to the

A.R.T. of barrel racing, versus a "style" of barrel racing that may be confined to certain types of horses. Time-honored riding theory creates a foundation and allows a horse to develop his individual style based on his individual abilities. What remains consistent is a horse who is supple, straight, strong, and capable of maintaining balance. Within certain confines that require some moves to be consistent and precise, there are others, after the horse has learned the basics, that allow the rider to be a little less rigid and allow the horse to show what he can do to make the task easier and more productive for himself. Balance and consistency still remain the goal. Adjusting rate points and pocket position all come into play as a horse develops his individual style.

Using "no plan is the plan" allows the rider to use skills and theory that allow for adjustments in training and competition procedures. The same task can be accomplished in many ways using a variety of skill exercises.

Anything good takes time. Foundation is critical to a horse, especially in an event where speed is so important. The mistake many riders make is that after a few good

Even though things are happening fast, remember to look and ride to the third cone position.

Use your outside leg and outside rein (outside neck rein if riding one-handed, as shown) to help the horse finish the turn and line up for a good approach to the next pocket point.

runs in the practice arena, they begin to enter competitions. It remains the rider's responsibility to know what level of competition his or her horse is ready for. The rider must know when to increase the pressure and when to back off. Once a horse's mind and confidence is blown, it is very difficult to bring either back.

Hint: A few weeks' vacation will freshen a horse's mind, relax his body, and nourish his enthusiasm. Each horse is an individual. Some horses need more time off during the year than others, and some can be worked more often than others. Correct management is the key in productive training and competition.

6

PROBLEM SOLVING

Accurately assessing the horse's performance will offer clues in resolving problems.

IF AT any time your horse develops performance problems, you should rule out a possible health issue before proceeding with further measures. When a horse who has been a consistent performer quits working, chronic and acute conditions are

If you have trouble picking your pocket point, a visual aid (here, the letter K on the fence in front of the rider) can help you look and ride to your pocket point.

both possibilities. The acute injuries are generally the easiest to identify. Subtle changes in way of going due to a chronic condition are more difficult.

This is where knowing what is "normal" for the horse, as discussed in Chapter 7, is critical to the role of a manager. Once you determine that the horse is sound, you should next consider your equipment. Chapter 4 can help you determine if equipment is causing discomfort and generating performance problems.

If you decide that performance could be enhanced by a change in competitive equipment, determine in which phase of the run—the approach, the rate, or the turn—problems occur. By evaluating each phase of the run, you can determine if a bit change, further skill development, or a combination of skill-building exercises, problem-specific corrections, and a bridle change are indicated.

Select a bridle that enhances communication. If a horse is running through the bit or fighting it, first check to see if the bit is properly adjusted, not pinching or causing some other discomfort. Next, make sure it is not a dental problem.

The goal is a positive correction. Using performance as a report card, determine the strengths and weaknesses of your horse's run. Accurately assessing performance will offer clues in resolving problems. Confirmation that the horse is sound and that the rider is correct in her balanced position and confident in the instruction indicates it may be time to utilize problem-specific corrections.

Remember the foundation snaffle-martingale is a tremendous resource in keeping the finished horse balanced and responsive and can be used to reinforce foundation at any stage of a horse's career.

Problems in the Approach

If the problem occurs in the approach, most often it results from the horse not remaining straight and balanced. This can be caused by the rider failing to obtain a good forward momentum—you cannot steer a horse who has no impulsion.

If you think the bit might be too intimidating by inhibiting forward motion, you might try a more neutral, short-shanked, minimal leverage bit, like my Tender Touch bit. If shoulder control is the issue, a bit that falls into the correction or lifter category would be appropriate. The combination bit also falls into the correction category. These bits usually combine a fuller purchase with longer shanks for more leverage and elevation.

Approach problem 1:
Difficulty in picking your point

Choosing the "pocket point," where you ask the horse to rate and prepare for the turn, can be a problem, especially for beginners. Unfortunately, even when you know where you want to turn, sometimes even an experienced rider lets the horse drift in, in effect "cheating" the pocket. This leads the horse to slice, or drop his shoulder into, the barrel.

To avoid this situation, pick the pocket point before the run begins. Looking straight beyond that point to the fence or some other extremely visible aid will help you maintain an upright, balanced body position and will help keep your approach honest. Stay aware of your rein and leg position. **Remember:** The barrel will not move, so learn to maintain the barrel in your peripheral vision and look directly at the pocket point.

The same technique applies to the second and third barrels. Because of the proximity of the arena fence, a lot of horses may be "scotchy" or overanticipate their approach. This causes a horse to slow down too much or too early at the barrels. If you are looking directly at the barrel instead of at a visual reference on the ground or fence, your body may subconsciously encourage the horse to anticipate the turn or cheat his position. For an honest approach, pick pocket points accurately,

One hand placed on the pommel creates a solid sensation that can discourage a horse from pulling excessively on the rider. Return to a normal hand position when the horse responds.

barrel, look beyond the point to select a visible aid. This is where you will look when you leave the start position. Pick visual aids to help you with the pocket points on the second and third barrels.

Remember: Successful turns start with successful, balanced approaches. Inaccurate approaches can create a domino effect. Slicing, V-ing (explained below), and shouldering may result.

Approach problem 2: Slicing a barrel

This problem results from an incorrect approach to the barrel. There are various causes.

If you sit and ask the horse to rate too early, he loses his momentum and closes in his pocket, his hip drifts out, and his shoulder drops toward the barrel. If he manages not to hit the barrel, he is still usually out of position. He will either run wide leaving the barrel because his approach was too close, or there will be a dead spot where he has to collect himself on the back side of the barrel. This is called "V-ing" a barrel, when a horse's turn has a V-shape that loses momentum at the point of the V, and results in compromised position.

The rider causes another variety of slicing by using too much indirect rein in order to try to maintain position. As you feel the horse shift his weight to drop into the barrel, you consequently use the outside rein in an attempt to pull the horse's nose and body away from the barrel. This causes the horse to drop his shoulder even farther toward the barrel, leaving his body arced in the opposite direction of the turn.

A more appropriate correction is using your legs to drive the horse forward, bumping with your inside leg to lift his shoulder and rib cage if needed, and using the inside rein to help elevate and balance the inside shoulder. The addition of the outside leg at the back cinch area can help keep the horse's rear underneath him. This position brings the horse's nose

ride to those points, ride both sides of your horse, and remember to see each barrel in your peripheral vision.

Walking the course on foot to select pocket points is an option if it's possible. Locate your individual start position in the alleyway or arena entrance, and then locate the first barrel marker. This will give you two fixed points: where you'll start and where the first barrel will sit.

Standing at the start position, pick your individual pocket point on the ground at the side of the first barrel. To help you make an effective approach to the first in and emphasizes the arc and balanced body position necessary to complete a smooth and efficient barrel turn.

This is a common problem in developing a seasoned horse. Reestablishing closer pocket points and shorter rate points as the horse develops his skills is crucial in avoiding and eliminating this problem.

In both types of slicing, careful attention should be given to visualizing the pocket points and selecting proper rate points. Since this is most often caused by the rider, the first corrections should involve developing your skills in determining pocket and rate points at all three barrels. The techniques described in the previous section on picking your point will be useful.

The shoulder in/shoulder out exercise helps resolve difficulties in maneuverability. Bits that help elevate the horse's shoulders, such as a lifters, solid-shanked chain bits, or combination bits, would complement the exercises.

Ride balanced in order to frame the horse between your legs and hands. Avoid rating too early, and avoid reining off with the outside rein. If necessary, use the inside rein to elevate the shoulder. Complement with the outside rein to emphasize the turning arc. Using the inside leg helps lift a dropped shoulder or the ribs. If the problem still exists, use arcing or breaking-off exercises.

Breaking off:
A problem-specific correction for slicing/shouldering

Indication: This corrective exercise helps resolve a shouldering or slicing problem when the horse is not responding to the attempts of the rider to reposition him.

Purpose: This exercise teaches the horse not to overanticipate a turn by dropping

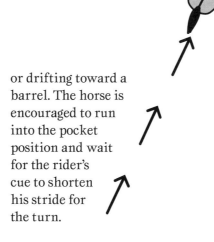

or drifting toward a barrel. The horse is encouraged to run into the pocket position and wait for the rider's cue to shorten his stride for the turn.

Mechanics:

Prerequisite to this exercise is competency in the figure-eight exercise.

Working first at a trot, approach the pocket, roll the inside wrist, and elevate the inside rein. Cue the horse to turn in the opposite direction, maintaining forward motion from the hindquarters and a reverse arc in the body or spine.

Make a complete circle *in the opposite direction*, come back to the pocket posi-

The breaking-off correction is designed to teach the horse not to anticipate the turn by dropping his shoulder toward a barrel and can be done at a trot, lope, or gallop. Just before the barrel turn, make a circle in the opposite direction, maintaining the body arc needed for the barrel turn. After circling, turn the barrel. It is critical to remember the horse must not pivot in this exercise. Impulsion from the hindquarters ensures forward movement.

Breaking-off correction: The horse drifts toward the barrel. The rider rolls her inside wrist to elevate inside rein and inside shoulder.

If at any time a horse develops problems, the rider needs to rule out a possible health issue before proceeding with further measures.

tion, then allow the horse to turn the barrel correctly with the arc repositioned toward the barrel.

Once you are proficient, this exercise can be done at a lope or gallop.

This exercise can be done at any place in the approach or at any point in the barrel turn. Use it wherever you determine the horse is dropping his shoulder or rib cage, overanticipating the turn, or drifting toward the barrel.

It should be repeated, in a single approach, *whenever* the rider feels the horse is dropping, drifting in, or taking away the turning space.

Maintain forward motion during the correction. Do not allow the horse to plant his hindquarters. This is not a spin or a pivot.

Arcing off is a variation of the breaking-off correction where the horse is asked to perform a portion of the latter before going to the next barrel. It can be used as a tuning strategy to remind the horse to

stay honest and wait for the rider's cue. It's used as a less extreme correction on the second and third barrels, but is not normally used on the first.

Problem 1: The rider arcs the horse in the wrong direction, possibly because she does not have a clear picture of what the correction looks like. She takes the horse's nose away from the barrel, therefore not giving the appropriate cue for a reverse arc.

Plan: Establish the correction in your mind. The exercise is designed to overemphasize shoulder elevation and to remind the horse not to drop into the turning rein.

Complete the exercise on foot to simulate the move you wish to complete on your horse.

Problem 2: The rider fails to maintain forward motion when completing the exercise.

Plan: Make sure you have forward mo-

Maintaining body arc to the right, the rider directs the horse to move forward in a circle to the left, away from the barrel.

The rider completes the circle to the left and returns to the barrel pocket. If the horse's position is correct (no dropped shoulders), he is allowed to complete the turn.

tion. If the horse fails to move his front legs, kick with both legs in the cinch area. Your body cue says: "Get off the rein; move forward and away from my leg."

Reestablish the forward motion before resuming the correction.

Problem 3: The rider holds both reins with equal pressure, not allowing the horse's body to move laterally.

Plan: Elevate the inside rein. Remember to relax the tension on the outside rein, opening the shoulder space, allowing the outside shoulder a place to move. The outside rein is only a guide. Restricting the outside rein restricts the horse's ability to move forward.

Bit resources: chain, lifter, long-shanked ultra.

The arcing-off correction is a variation of the breaking-off correction used primarily on the second and third barrels to remind the horse not to overanticipate the turn. At the rate point the horse is cued to turn in the opposite direction while maintaining a reverse arc. Instead of turning a complete circle, the horse moves down the arena to the next barrel without turning the previous one.

Third Barrel

bit offers little vertical control and is often overused in barrel racing.

Failure by the rider to ask for the rate

The rider needs to be methodical in cueing for rate at each of the three barrels. Consistent cueing assists the horse in shortening his stride and prepares him for a balanced and precise turn. Two hands on the reins help the rider to balance and collect the horse at the rate position.

Failure of the horse to respond to the rider's request for rate

The rider needs to be precise in the technique used for cueing for the rate. (Refer to Chapter 4 for technique on stopping.) If the horse continues to blow by barrels, he is not responding to the rider. To analyze the possible cause the rider should:

- Evaluate possible health concerns, dental issues, injuries, etc.
- Check the bridle for correct fit, and readjust if necessary. **Remember:** Raising the bit, creating a more defined wrinkle in the corners of the mouth, and/or tightening the chin strap can increase the response. A solid bar curb bit might get better results.
- Check the tie-down adjustments and alternatives. Determine if adjusting the length of the tie-down is required. If necessary, consider an alternate type, such as a rope, cable, or chain noseband tie-down.
- Consider your bridle options. If a change is indicated, bits that can enhance rate are the polo, chain, and hackamore bit. A quick-stop should be used for reinforcing correction only.

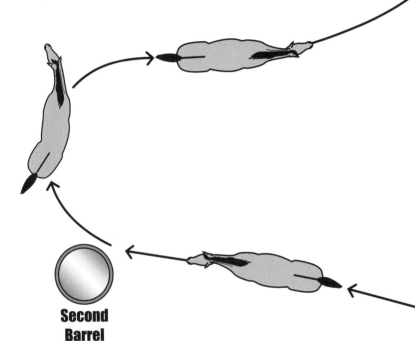

Second Barrel

Problems in the Rate

Problems that occur in the rate phase generally relate to:

- Lack of stopping or backing-up skills
- Failure of the rider to systematically ask for the rate
- Failure of the horse to respond to the rider's request for rate
- Ineffective bridle
- Failure to identify soreness in the horse's back, hocks, etc.

Difficulties that occur in the rate phase of the run can be approached by using bits that offer more vertical or speed control. Bits that enhance rate include the polo, chain, or combination. The more solid the bit, the more vertical the control. A gag-type

If the horse does not respond to the rider's cue, work on the skill-building exercises that helped teach the horse to stop. If the horse can't stop away from the barrels, it is unlikely that he will respond to rate during a barrel run. The problem is compounded once speed is added.

If the horse doesn't stop or collect when cued by the rider, a problem-specific correction is needed. The severity of the problem determines which exercise the rider should choose. The rollback is a good problem-specific correction for a more advanced horse. A green horse will normally respond to backing-up reinforcement.

Backing: A problem-specific correction to reinforce rate

Indication: Backing can be used to reinforce rate and collection. It is useful for horses needing a gentle reminder to shift their weight off the forehand, or for horses who are just starting their barrel work.

Purpose: Backing aids in strengthening the horse's loin area and shifting the weight off the forehand and onto the hindquarters.

Mechanics:
- Lope or trot to the barrel, sit down, and ask for a collected stop.
- Back the horse several steps. Try to back the horse onto his inside turning hock, using more inside rein and outside leg for this position.
- Allow the horse to settle for several seconds before asking him to proceed forward around the barrel.
- During the backing exercise remember to stimulate movement in the horse's feet and entire body with your legs and hands.

Rollback: A problem-specific correction for reinforcing rate

Indication: This correction can be used for each of the three barrels. The correction may need to be repeated until the horse responds. If the horse does not respond after two or three attempts, return to appropriate skill-building exercises and remove the pattern work from the correction.

Purpose: This exercise is used to estab-

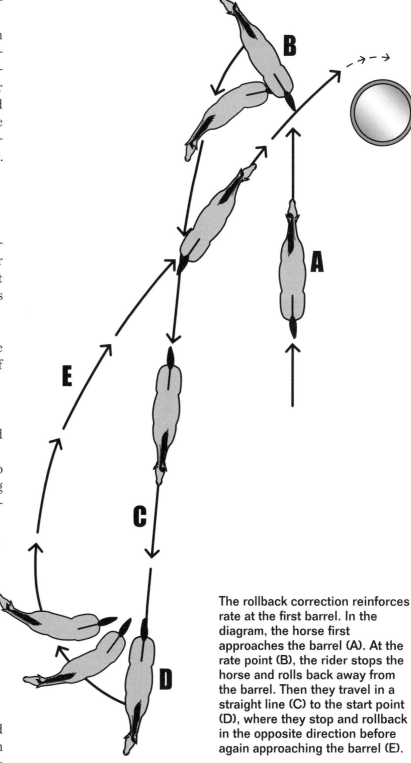

The rollback correction reinforces rate at the first barrel. In the diagram, the horse first approaches the barrel (A). At the rate point (B), the rider stops the horse and rolls back away from the barrel. Then they travel in a straight line (C) to the start point (D), where they stop and rollback in the opposite direction before again approaching the barrel (E).

lish a consistent response to the rider's request for stop/rate and collection.

Mechanics:
- Approach the first barrel. Cue for rate, using correct sequence and body position.

Rollback correction to reinforce rate: The rider sits deep in the saddle, says whoa, and increases rein contact to cue the horse to shorten his stride and stop.

The horse is backed a few steps to help him shift his weight off the forehand and onto the hindquarters.

The rider rolls the horse away from the barrel (here, to the left) and sends him in a straight line back to the start point.

The rider stops the horse at the start point, which in this case is the fence.

To help position the horse for the correct lead, the rider rolls the horse back in the opposite direction from the first rollback (here, to the right) and heads back to the barrel.

At the pocket position, the rider repeats the cue for rate. If the horse shortens his stride with little effort, continue around the barrel. If not, repeat the exercise.

- Maintain solid rein contact until the horse stops.
- Back the horse a few steps to take his weight off the forehand. Make sure to position him on his outside turning hock before requesting the rollback.
- Roll back *away* from the barrel using direct rein to start the turn and reinforcement from the outside rein and leg to send horse in the reverse direction.
- Trot or lope, depending on the level of training, back to the arena fence. Use the fence as an aid to help shift the horse's weight off his forehand, before asking for another stop.
- Set up and once again roll back toward the direction of the approaching turn, right to right barrel, left to left barrel.
- If loping or galloping, ask for the correct lead.
- Approach the pocket position once again.
- Sit, say whoa, and ask for another stop.

Circling correction: If a problem is felt at any time during a turn …

Most horse problems are caused by inconsistent training programs, mixed cues, and/or unrecognized injury.

• Repeat the exercise until the horse produces a satisfactory response before continuing on the pattern.

Problem: The rider fails to complete the correct sequence when requesting rate. Most often the rider forgets to sit and roll the pelvis first. Instead she first picks up on the reins, causing the horse to resist by stiffening, elevating his head, and hollowing his back. The horse's weight remains on his forehand. The response is a stiff-legged, roughly executed stop.

Plan: The rider must remember to:
• Sit first and cue for a stop with your body weight.
• Reinforce with a verbal whoa.
• Using two hands, increase contact on the reins until the horse responds.
• If the horse continues to push through the bit, a firm seesaw hand motion can help lighten him and produce a response.

Bit resources: polo, chain correction, hackamore bit, quick stop

Note: Horses should lightly anticipate the rate. This attention gives the rider confidence to ride hard and aggressively into the rate position.

The rider can practice rate at any time during the approach to verify the horse's responsiveness. It is not out of the question to practice rate 50 feet before the turn or anywhere in between. In fact, I like to ask for rate and collection as I travel down the side fence between the no stop/no start pattern. The goal is responsiveness anywhere, any speed, any time. Remember the importance of your foundation training away from the barrel pattern.

Problems in the Turn

Problems in the turn are usually related to the horse having too much or too little bend. If a horse is too stiff, a gag-type bit offers more lateral control for the turn. Be aware that a gag bit may offer too much bend, allowing the rider to pull the nose too much, forcing the horse onto his front end. This will sacrifice rate and cause the horse to step out behind or to bow out wide in a turn. If a horse has too much bend, try to stiffen him with a solid-sided bit, or perhaps even a hackamore bit designed for lateral control.

Circling: A problem-specific correction for pivoting on the front end

Indication: This correction helps when a horse displays difficulties maintaining impulsion and correct body alignment in

… remove the pressure of the turn by expanding the turning position into a neutral 40-foot circle around the barrel.

Once the horse is relaxed and balanced …

… tighten the circle, turn the barrel, and return to the pattern.

Double-down correction: To create a time-out option from a potentially volatile situation for either horse or rider, the rider pulls the horse's head firmly toward her knee and circles five or six times. Bumping with the inside leg toward the back cinch encourages the horse to free up his hindquarters. Excellent for a horse who lacks focus on the rider, this movement through the hindquarters defuses the horse's ability to back or rear.

his turn. He plants his front legs, which causes his hindquarters to move sideways.

Purpose: Circling takes the pressure off the horse and helps the rider create impulsion and balance as the horse circles the barrels.

Mechanics:
- Lope or gallop to the barrel, making sure the horse is framed between your hands and legs.
- Sit, rate, and ask for one barrel turn.
- If you identify a problem in the turn, circle the barrel again, maintaining the lope or gallop, and increase the size of the circle to approximately 40 feet in diameter with the barrel exactly in the center, effectively removing the pressure the barrel may present. Use the larger circles to help rebalance and reposition the horse.
- Make sure the horse strides forward. To increase his stride, bump the horse with both legs at the cinch area.
- Continue to circle the barrel at a lope or gallop, until the horse relaxes and moves at a consistent speed on the correct lead, framed between your hands and legs. If the problem of pivoting around the front end persists, a slap on the outside hip with your hand, over-and-under, or training reins may be required to move the horse forward.
- Once you feel the horse's front and rear are moving with balanced forward motion, tighten the turn around the barrel (as small a circle as your horse is comfortable with in his stage of training) and then allow him to go on to the next barrel.
- Do not continue circling after the horse relaxes and responds correctly. Tightening your turn and going on to the next barrel removes the pressure and results in the reward.

Problem: The rider has difficulty maintaining the size of the circle and timing the use of the rein, hand, or over-and-under.

Plan:
- Visualize and establish a consistent, even circle. Imagine the barrel as the hub of your 40-foot circle.
- Ride two-handed with the horse's body framed between your hands and legs. Use your legs to balance and stabilize the horse's rib cage and forward motion.
- Prepare to use a reinforcing aid, training rein, or over-and-under as necessary.
- If necessary, reinforce the horse's body position. If he is dropping in the circle, bump with your leg on the inside shoulder and hip. If he drifts to the outside of the circle, use your outside rein and leg.

Bit resources: Tender Touch, gag, Short Ultra, chain. These bits help create forward motion and a balanced position.

The skill-building exercises that aid in strengthening barrel turns are the corkscrew and the all right/all left exercise. These are effective ways to remove pressures and build skills.

Pivoting exercises, such as spins and 360-degree rotations, help develop the quick moves a horse utilizes on the backside of the barrel, which in turn produce a quickness in the turn.

Scoring the Arena-Sour Horse

The sour horse doesn't want to enter the arena. He has probably been frustrated and confused by inconsistent training methods on the barrel pattern and intimidated by the pressure of the competition. The horse feels he can avoid the confrontation if he refuses to go in the arena.

This type of problem usually comes from inexperience of the rider. It is helpful to practice entering the arena in a relaxed manner. Score the horse by petting him on the neck and rump as you ride in to help restore his confidence. The rider should *remain* relaxed. If the over-and-under can be used to ask the horse to move forward, be cautious not to pull on the reins at the same time. This inhibits forward motion and sends mixed signals.

Scoring the horse in and out of the gate or alley area is similar to a roper scoring his rope horse in the box. Because of the rider's apprehensions, both areas might be stressful locations to a horse. Loosening the cinch and dismounting in the arena, whenever possible, is a good habit to reward a horse. Most horse problems are rider-related and reinforced by inconsistent training programs, mixed cues, overly tense and nervous riders, and inability of the rider to identify horse soreness.

Double-down: A problem-specific correction for a refusal to move forward

Indication: This correction is used when a horse fails to respond or resists the rider's commands. The maneuver can also reestablish the horse's attention on the rider. It is similar to a time-out.

Purpose: The double-down gives the horse the option to produce a correct response. It provides a positive discipline and time-out zone to buffer an explosive or unresponsive situation, such as failure to move forward or backward, sulking, possible rearing, or lack of attention to the rider

Mechanics: At the point when the horse fails to respond—for instance, to the request of the rider to move forward—the rider should:
- Pull the horse's head firmly toward your knee in order to confine the horse's movement to a small circle.
- Circle, at least five or six rotations, to regain the horse's attention.

The severity of the problem determines which exercise the rider should choose.

- If necessary, use your inside leg to bump in the area of the horse's flank to free the horse's hindquarters and encourage lateral movement.
- If the horse's front legs are not moving, possibly because he is pivoting on his front end, use both your legs in the cinch area to move the horse forward into the small circle.
- After five or six circles, allow the horse an opportunity to respond to your initial command.
- If the horse refuses to respond, repeat the double-down correction.
- As soon as the horse attempts to respond to the requested move, praise and reward. Remember the importance of "consistent reward and discipline." Do not carry a grudge. Remember that each and every difficult situation provides an opportunity to train.

Problem 1: The rider fails to move the horse's body in a forward circle during the correction. The rider fails to firmly take the horse's nose to the inside to make him uncomfortable.

Plan:

- The correction must be done with motion. Use both feet in the cinch area to keep the front feet moving, and use your inside leg in the flank area to keep the hind feet moving.
- Pull the horse's nose toward your knee. The direction of the circle doesn't matter; the movement and discipline of the exercise are important.
- Complete five or six circles, since the number of circles make the correction uncomfortable and provide time for the horse to refocus on the rider.

Problem 2: The rider gets angry.

Plan:

- Remember that anger never accomplishes anything. Allow yourself a time-out.
- Don't get mad; get even. Make the right move (responding to your request) easy for the horse (stop circling), and the wrong move (refusal to respond) difficult (keep circling).
- The round pen is a good time-out area for both horse and rider.
- An option for a horse who has a tendency to be barrel sour is to temporarily work him in the opposite direction on the barrel pattern. When you switch which barrel you go to first, it sometimes brings the horse back to listening to your cues.

Whips and Spurs

Spurs and whips can create more problems for inexperienced riders than they can solve. It's hard even for experienced riders to use spurs effectively without inadvertently gouging the horse.

First, the horse should be asked to move forward by pressure from your thighs and calves. If necessary, reinforce the move by using your heels.

Spurs are best used to assist with placement of the horse's body. Overuse or incorrect use of spurs can actually shorten the horse's stride or cause him stress, resulting in tail-wringing and possibly urination during a work.

Over-and-unders and whips, when responsibly used and correctly applied, are more helpful to extend the stride. Ask the horse to move or stride forward when his front end comes off the ground. If you use the whip or over-and-under when the front end is down, it shortens his stride and inhibits his forward flow.

In Summary

Keeping them tuned

Remember that the all lefts/all rights exercise and corkscrew exercise are alternate skills that can be practiced instead of the cloverleaf pattern. Try to make the arena work fun, creative, and interesting for both horse and rider.

Keeping horses working is often more difficult than training them in the first place. It is important to build a working relationship and respect between horse and rider. This respect creates a bond that will carry horse and rider through the stressful situations that will be encountered in competition. Consistent reward and discipline help reinforce the horse's idea of exactly what is expected from his performance.

Do not underestimate the resource of the training snaffle and martingale in helping to keep even the best of athletes tuned and in peak performance. When properly used the snaffle helps keep a horse light and responsive to the rider's cues.

Evaluating performance

Letting each run be a report card is a good and productive tool in evaluating strengths and weaknesses in training and performance. Train yourself to remember and be able to access the feel of each run. This will allow you to build on the positive and strengthen the weak points that show up with speed under the pressure of competition.

Maintaining a happy horse

It is important to keep the horse's movements free and fluid. Remember not to overwork your barrel horse. Exercise and condition him outside the arena as much as possible. A long trail ride is a good break for both horse and rider.

As human athletes, none of us excel every time we compete. A horse is no different. We are all entitled to have a few off days. Consistency—the ability to make each run count by riding and placing our horse in a balanced position so that he has the opportunity to excel in performance—is the goal.

For a seasoned horse, it's good to minimize the barrel work at home. Just keep your winner happy, tuned, and conditioned. For a young horse, conditioning and training are equally as important. It

is not out of the question to have a conditioning workout followed by arena work four or five times per week to help develop skill exercises and pattern work.

Keep in mind that horses have shorter attention spans than humans. Adapt your conditioning and training program to the individual horse. More than one training session can be accomplished in a riding period. Remember to remove the pressure and take the horse off task in between sessions for a mental break and reward.

Our goal is to leave the arena once the training or tuning session has been productively accomplished. Take caution not to overwork or drill irresponsibly on the barrel pattern. The skill exercises in this book are designed not only to train horses, but also to train rider positions and consistencies, and at the same time to reinforce the skills required on the barrel pattern.

Final thought

It is very important that the relationship between the rider and the horse be productive and realistic. In order to create a positive focus, riders need to remind themselves that it takes time to learn the horsemanship skills necessary to develop an equine athlete. The rider must not allow stages of development to be discouraging.

It's also true that not every horse and rider combination will hit it off or get along well together. Call it a personality clash. Sometimes it is a matter of the horse's temperament not matching the rider's schedule, such as when a horse needs to be ridden and handled every day but the owner can only devote a short time each week.

I have seen situations where a horse works for one person and not for another. If an impossible situation becomes obvious, the smart rider should get out before either the rider, the horse, or both get hurt or discouraged. The bottom line is enjoyment and safety. If you can't get either of these, it may be time for a change.

7

CARE AND CONDITIONING

Establish a health care team to maintain your horse's health and productivity.

IT IS easiest to understand your role in the care and conditioning of your equine partner if you view yourself as a manager of his well-being. As a manager, you are responsible for your horse's health and conditioning.

It is also the manager's responsibility to provide certain aspects of care and to be knowledgeable about when to access care from professionals. The establishment of a professional health care team, consisting of veterinarians, equine dentists, farriers, and chiropractors, is essential to maintaining the equine athlete's health and productivity.

Areas of responsibility that require a working knowledge on the part of the manager include:

- Identification of your horse's baseline
- Conditioning
- Nutrition
- Grooming
- Hoof care
- Deworming and vaccinations
- Dental care

Time spent riding out of the arena will help keep your horse mentally fresh and physically fit.

Identification of Your Horse's Baseline

Part of your responsibility as your horse's manager is to identify what is "normal" for him. Knowledge of his way of going, vital signs (temperature, heart and respiratory rates), eating and drinking patterns, swellings, lumps and bumps, and even what his gut sounds are like under normal circumstances are the keys for making decisions pertaining to care.

Knowing how to take a horse's vital signs is important. The ability to compare readings taken when a problem arises and compare them to those obtained under normal circumstances will help you determine the severity of the problem. This is very important when the care of your regular veterinarian is not available, and you must provide a clear history for a veterinarian not familiar with the horse.

I encourage riders to speak with their veterinarians about the following and to keep these important facts in a small journal stored in a vet kit:

- Temperature: normal range 99.5 to 100.5 degrees Fahrenheit
- Respiration: normal range 6 to 20 breaths per minute
- Pulse rate: normal range 28 to 44 beats per minute
- Skin pinch (for evaluating dehydration): normal recovery 1 to 2 seconds
- Capillary refill time: normal recovery 1 to 2 seconds.

Being informed about the specifics of your horse's health will help you with daily planning and the ability to make the right choices should an emergency arise.

Conditioning

Performance problems and injuries are often caused by an inadequate conditioning program. Fatigued muscles allow relaxation of ligaments and tendons. This in turn enhances the chances of injuries

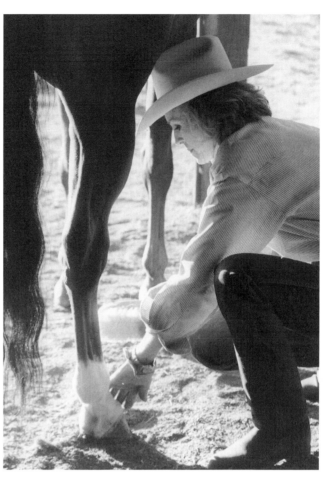

Check your horse every day for signs of injury, swelling, or lameness.

to joints, ligaments, and tendons, and even of bone fractures. Further compounding the potential problem are the traditional inconsistencies in ground, arena conditions, and warm-up location.

This being true for the mature horse, it is an even greater consideration for the competitive equine less than 5 years old. A young horse has an immature skeletal structure and is at increased risk for injury. Strict attention to the conditioning program of young horses should increase your chances of preserving their soundness.

Managing the conditioning program, therefore, is equally important as the training program. Training schools a horse for competition, while conditioning prepares the horse physically to withstand the rigors of the contest. Not only does a well-conditioned horse have a better chance of winning, he has a better chance of staying sound. Considering how

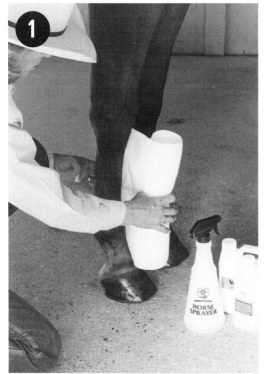
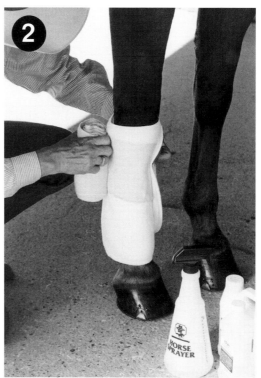

A standing bandage helps support your horse's legs during travel or stall rest. 1: You can first apply a leg brace or liniment and rub to stimulate blood flow. Then lay the edge of a cotton wrap along the inside of the leg, as shown. Wrap from inside around the front to outside—clockwise on right legs, counterclockwise on left legs. 2: Apply a flannel bandage over the cotton. Start at the top, work down to the ankle, then work back up the leg. Keep the bandage wrinkle-free to prevent bandage bows. 3: A completed wrap should be smooth and provide even pressure. Be careful not to wrap too tightly, however, as that can cause serious problems.

difficult it is to make a winner, it's important to do everything possible to preserve his soundness and longevity.

Once a horse is trained and seasoned, his work program should be switched so that conditioning is a primary focus of physical activity. A horse should be in good shape, with workouts between five to nine miles, three to five days per week. The precise distance will vary with the fortitude of the individual.

A typical five-mile workout would include a one-mile warm up, one mile of trotting, one mile of galloping, and a two-mile cool off. The trotting and galloping distances can be increased as the horse's condition develops. If there is no gauge for distance available—if you can only ride in an arena, for example—estimate that it takes about 45 minutes to one hour for a five-mile workout. A gradual build-up to a 10-minute lope is included.

This conditioning program will be modi-fied once a horse goes on the road to a lot of competitions. The program during an active season will be maintenance, walking, long-trotting, and a little galloping.

The cool-off portion of exercising and competition is important for the equine athlete in order to prevent injuries and soreness. It seems to take the muscles about 20 minutes of walking to recover from a strenuous exercise, even though the horse may look cool and is breathing normally. Don't put him away before allowing for muscle recovery, or he runs the risk of developing muscle soreness and stiffness.

I want to stress that any conditioning program, if mismanaged, can be as hard on an out-of-shape horse as the training program can be. The horse who has not been ridden or conditioned for six months will very likely take three to four months to get back into peak physical condition. A horse in decent physical condition can peak in 30 to 60 days. Once condition is lost in an

People all over the country ask me about Seven, my partner for three of my four National Finals Rodeos. This photo was taken during his retirement, when I continued to carefully monitor his health and condition. Seven was put down April 1999 and is buried at my home in Lockeford, Calif. Seven was honored with a model horse replica produced by Stone Horses.

older horse, it is even harder to restore.

Each horse is an individual and must be conditioned accordingly. Studies have been done on conditioning race horses and endurance horses, but just how one should go about conditioning a horse to give everything he has for an 18-second barrel racing run is up to the owner or trainer.

We don't want our horses as fresh as race horses, or as flat as some performance show horses. On the other hand, we don't need them in the same condition as an endurance horse. We do need them toned and attentive. A younger horse needs time off to allow for mental relaxation and recuperation. A horse may take too much time to "ride down" in order to achieve mental attentiveness, if he is too fit or fed too well early in his training.

Sometimes a seasoned horse will gradually get "scotchy," especially after a summer of competition. He will be in top condition in the spring, but at the end of the summer season, he's a little sour, a little sore, and probably burnt-out on travel and barrel racing. He is not giving all he can, especially when he leaves the third barrel. In a timed event, the stopwatch is a gauge that doesn't lie.

I find taking this individual to the track and sprinting him is helpful. If this conditioned horse is not making competitive runs during the week, I'll add what race horse trainers call a "work" every seven to ten days: walk a mile, trot one-half mile, pick up a lope for one-fourth to one-half mile, and then sprint the horse—*ask him for everything he has*—for approximately 250 yards, then back off to a gallop, and ease down to a walk to thoroughly cool him out. On these days he is exercised harder, but for less time and less distance. This "work" increases his lung capacity, tightens and tones muscles, and helps increase bone density.

Even though a horse is making a lot of runs, he may gradually lose his wind without the longer distance workouts. Letting your horse swim for a week in an equine swimming pool is a great way to "freshen" him up. This gives him a break from the routine, and it's good for his aerobic conditioning. Ponying also provides a productive resource to maintain condition and keep a horse limber and refreshed.

Remember: Conditioning is not an overnight process. It requires patience, intelligence, and consistency.

Nutrition

In caring for the equine athlete, consistency is important. It is also important to feed each horse according to his individual needs.

It is sometimes difficult to control hay quality while traveling, but staying consistent in the grain ration is possible. I suggest a good quality, oat-based sweet feed. Often I cut this mixture with one-half whole oats and one-half premixed

Each horse is an individual and must be conditioned according to his individual needs.

feed. Purina Mills is a manufacturer of consistent products that are available throughout the country.

Research shows that low-carbohydrate and high-fat content in feed is conducive in assisting with peak performance and condition. A rule of thumb I use is that the percentage of carbohydrate in the feed should be 12 percent or lower and the fat content 12 percent or higher. I find the lower protein level and higher fat content help maintain condition and nutritional levels without getting a horse high.

Remember to feed the individual according to his individual needs. Grain may not be a prerequisite to optimum nutrition if good quality hay is available. In fact some horses are fed too much concentrate, which affects their ability to focus on the rider or task at hand. A good rule of thumb is more work, more grain; less work, less grain.

Vitamin supplements can be used as a responsible resource to enhance the overall nutritional status.

A shiny, healthy-looking haircoat can usually be maintained by giving higher fat in the diet. Corn and soy oil are excellent resources for fat. Another resource for fat is rice bran products. Marketed with a guarantee of 19 percent fat, rice bran products produce excellent coat condition, and their fat content supplies reserve energy. The bran might be more palatable than the corn oil. This product can help maintain condition on a horse who has difficulty gaining weight.

Managing nutrition includes adjusting the feed as requirements change. If the horse is being hauled a lot of miles and making a lot of runs, or if the horse warms up flat and doesn't seem to have a lot of life, an increase in his grain ration may be indicated. First review vital signs and make a head-to-hoof check to rule out illness. A thorough evaluation would include having your veterinarian obtain blood tests to check for anemia or other abnormalities. Correct management and trainer awareness allows utilization of input from various equine professionals to maximize the horse's efficiency.

If the horse begins to get high (lacks focus) or if riding requirements decrease, reduce his grain. Do not feed a horse too much "hot feed" (grains high—usually more than 12 percent—in energy-boosting carbohydrates and proteins) unless he is being exercised hard. If he isn't working and his grain ration is not adjusted, he could be prone to tying up or even laminitis.

At home give the horse a salt block for free-choice use. On the road, I advise adding one tablespoon of Lite Salt to his grain to help keep him drinking water. Other options to avoid dehydration on the road or in extremely humid weather are prepackaged electrolyte powders or pastes.

Shoeing

Understanding hoof structure will help you manage your horse's hoof care.

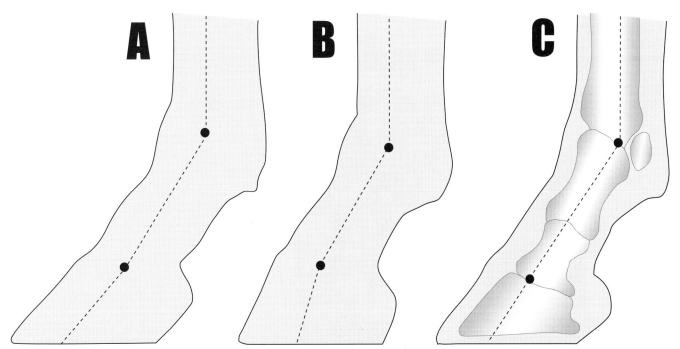

A: Long toe-low heel configuration can lead to tendon and ligament injuries. B: Too vertical of a hoof angle puts excess weight on the toe. C: The angle of the hoof should match the slope of the pastern.

First look at the hoof axis, or angle, in the accompanying illustrations. Illustrations A and B each display an axis that will increase the horse's chances for ligament and tendon injury. Illustration A shows a long toe-low heel configuration, which predisposes a horse to a variety of tendon and ligament injuries. Illustration B shows a hoof with too vertical of an angle, putting excess weight on the toe.

Illustration C shows that the angle of the hoof conforms to the slope of the pastern. Maintaining the integrity of this angle when shoeing is the goal.

Keeping the hoof level is another area of consideration. The horse should be shod so that the hoof hits flat. One side of the hoof should not touch down before the other. An unlevel hoof produces increased strain on joints, ligaments, and tendons.

A young barrel horse can be started in traditional rim shoes. One of their advantages is traction. The best traction is dirt against dirt, so don't worry when the rims are filled with dirt.

If a problem later shows up and the horse needs a change of shoes, a modification can be made. Horses will also often go through stages where they need different shoes during different phases of their training. A variety of shoes are available. It is part of the equine manager's role to be familiar with the options and to work with the farrier to make the most effective choice.

For example, I had a horse who had a tendency to clip himself high inside his hind legs during turns. The inside hind leg would hit the outside hind leg during a powerful, high-speed turn. My farrier corrected this by putting a trailer with a cork on the outside of each back shoe. That gave the horse more support in his turns and cured the slippage.

Some time later, after running on a lot of hard ground, I discovered the corks were beginning to make the horse sore in his hocks and back. They were fine in soft ground, but caused too much drag on hard ground. We then went to steel polo plates and removed the cork. They worked well for a while, but the particular horse was so powerful that they did not offer enough wall support. I switched back to a regular rim shoe and the problem did not recur.

The polo plate is similar to a rim shoe,

Proper hoof angle will enhance your horse's athletic performance.

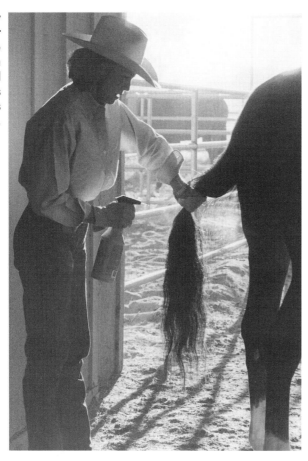

Spray conditioner helps remove tangles from manes and tails, as well as making coats shiny and soft.

Consistent dewormings and vaccinations put horses in top health.

but the inside rim is higher than the outside rim. This differs from the barrel racing plate, which has a higher outside rim. Because the polo plate has an inside rim it reduces the chance of the horse hurting himself if he happens to overreach. To further help prevent overreaching, the back toes can be squared off.

Different shoes work for different horses. The surfaces you may run on will vary from deep heavy ground to hard slick surfaces. Unless it is an important event, like a year-end finals, a futurity, etc., avoid shoes that are geared for only one type of running surface. I advise staying away from corked and exotic shoes unless it is advised for a short term correction or condition.

For increased traction a farrier can cup out the feet. However, I do not like to overdo the cupping. For example, race horses really have their feet cupped out, but they are usually running on nicely manicured ground. Barrel horses, especially rodeo

barrel horses, might have to be warmed up on gravel or pavement; a deeply cupped hoof is more susceptible to stone bruises because the sole is thinner.

Trimming a horse's toe back can help with a quicker breakover in his stride. Consequently, he can break away from a barrel more quickly. However, if you get those feet set too straight, it can shorten the stride. It's a very fine line. I prefer toes filed back "a hair," rather than left out long. The slope of the hoof should still conform to the slope of the pastern.

Make sure the shoes are "set full." Some farriers will put a slightly smaller shoe on a hoof, to avoid any "overhang." This can gradually make the foot smaller which leads to contracted heels. That's just one more problem to have to overcome. **Remember:** no foot, no horse. The horse needs all the support a shoe can offer.

When hauling it might be a good idea to carry an extra set of shoes shaped especially for your horse by your personal farrier. This eliminates having to have new shoes shaped by someone unfamiliar with your horse.

A good farrier should allow for the horse's individual conformation. Remember not to correct the hoof too much. The horse should be shod as he stands. Depending on the individual horse, shoeing should be on a five- to eight-week schedule.

Clearly, most of us are not farriers. It is therefore essential that you have confidence in your farrier. The ability to develop a good working relationship with your farrier as well as with other equine professionals is your responsibility. It is essential that the equine professionals selected work as a team. Just as it takes a pit crew to work on a race car, it takes a team to manage your horse's peak performance.

Deworming and Vaccinations

Equines need to be on an effective, consistent deworming program—every two to

Spraying on a solution of alcohol and water can help remove sweat after a workout. It also works well as a stimulating leg brace after a competition or workout.

These are the items in my grooming kit.

three months. Alternating between paste and tube worming is an option, but with the new improved pastes on the market, one could probably control parasites with pastes alone. Check on the thoroughness of your deworming program by taking fecal samples to a veterinarian for analysis. Daily dewormers have proven very effective, especially in areas where horses run a risk of high infestation.

In spring get the appropriate immunizations for your geographic area, which often include vaccinations for rhinopneumonitis, influenza, and tetanus. Follow up with vaccination boosters suggested by your veterinarian.

I give a flu shot to any horse who will be hauled a lot. I think it is especially important to give the flu shot to a young horse because he hasn't built up the resistance that an older horse might have.

Have your horse's teeth checked at least once a year by a veterinarian who specializes in equine dentistry. Veterinary studies show that growth, nutrition, comfort, and performance can be enhanced dramatically by modifying and managing the shape of the teeth. The simplest way to do this is by floating, or filing down sharp points on the teeth. Your vet can also advise you if your horse needs to have his wolf teeth, which can interfere with the bit, removed.

Equine dentistry has gone far beyond simple floating. Discoveries are showing that many performance faults can be addressed by correcting dental problems. If a horse's condition drops off, if he isn't eating like he should, or if he starts fighting a bit he used to work in, he could need some dental work.

A horse's medical issues should be treated as you would treat those of any loved one. Irreversible damage can be done by diagnosing and treating your horse without the aid of a veterinarian. Maintaining routine health care and contacting a veterinarian when emergencies arise is critical to your horse's well-being.

HAULING AND WINNING

Once you begin hauling, keeping you and your horse physically fit and mentally prepared are the keys to winning.

ONCE YOU decide to begin hauling to competitions, you should consider how to provide for the comfort, safety, health, and emergency care of your horse while on the road.

Being aware of the common illnesses that affect horses is important. This knowledge will help you plan and make decisions about your hauling arrangements. The most common ailments that occur when a horse is hauled are colic, dehydration, and respiratory infection, often referred to as shipping fever. The most common emergency from injury is excessive blood loss.

Frequently identified causes of colic are

sudden changes in diet or a decrease in water consumption. Respiratory infections can be brought on by the stress of hauling, with road fumes, dust in the trailer, and dehydration compounding the problem. Dehydration can be caused by excessive fluid loss (sweating), in hot and/or humid climates, or failure of the horse to drink an adequate amount of water. Wounds that involve arteries or large lacerations can cause excessive blood loss.

Each of these conditions requires emergency care from a veterinarian. All are potential complications of hauling a horse. Even with precautions, accidents occur, but being prepared will provide

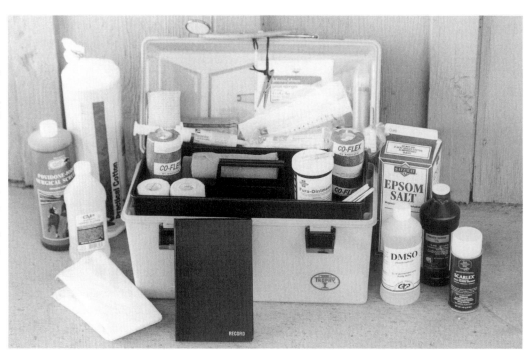

My vet kit, for general and emergency use, includes: thermometer with string and clip, antibacterial ointment and spray, a roll of cotton, sheet cotton for wraps, Vetrap™, Elasticon, Telfa pads, Kling, 4 by 4-inch bandages, tape, tongue depressors, Betadine scrub and/or solution, a large syringe for flushing wounds, epsom salt, and a flashlight.

peace of mind when emergencies arise because you know you did everything possible to prevent them.

Comfort and Safety

One of the first considerations is planning the horse's diet while he is away from home. The goal is to avoid changes in diet and provide consistency in his food source. You can keep his diet consistent by bringing his food from home. If you purchase hay or grain on the road, make sure to get as close to the regular feed as possible.

When on the road, plan your rest stops around the horse's usual feeding times. Every effort should be made to stay as close to the horse's regular schedule as possible. It is strongly advised to carry an ample water supply from home for drinking or emergency care.

Preparing the horse for his haul might include preloading him with electrolytes, administering a bran mash two to three days before shipping, adding Kool-Aid to his drinking water one week before you depart, or even administering mineral oil along with the bran. The specific regime for your horse will be based on the individual and how accustomed he is to trailering. Where he is going and how long he will be gone will help determine your decisions in this area. Consult your veterinarian for the best plan for your horse.

The veterinarian can also make sure the horse is current on his immunizations. Be sure to discuss the requirements of the location you are hauling to. Get the horse's shots updated several weeks before you leave to allow time for his immunity to build up. Don't forget to have a current Coggins test certificate, health certificate, and brand inspection slip, which are required by many states.

Make sure your horse can load and unload easily before you leave home. The time spent training a horse to load at home is the best insurance for avoiding difficulties and injuries on the road.

Be sure that your trailer provides your horse enough room to stand comfortably. Shavings can be used for absorption; spraying shavings with mineral oil cuts down on dust.

Trailer Safety

There are a variety of commercial shipping wraps available that provide protection for the horse. All four legs should be protected, with the wraps covering the pastern and coronet band, the areas most prone to injury during hauling. A support wrap can be applied if you are experienced in its application. **Remember:** An improperly applied leg wrap can cause tendon injuries, even bows.

Have blankets on hand for changes in climates. It is important for the horse not to get too hot inside the trailer, so make sure there is plenty of airflow through the trailer. If your horse is cold, put a blanket on him instead of closing all the windows. If you do travel with your horse blanketed, check him frequently to make sure he does not get hot.

When selecting a trailer, regardless of the type, be sure it provides enough room for your horse to stand comfortably and shift his weight. A trailer should be equipped with vents and windows to

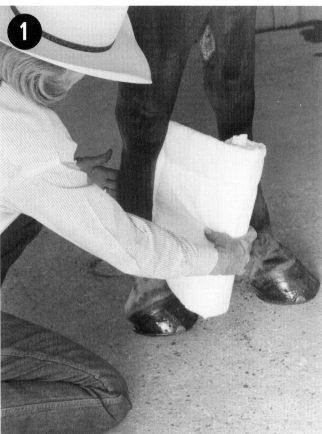

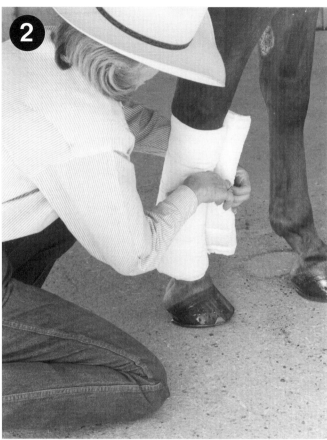

I advise using shipping wraps when hauling your horse. There are many varieties of shipping boots and wraps. If using wraps, start the wrap on the inside of the leg.

Wrap clockwise on the right leg and counter-clockwise on the left leg. Another way to think of this: Wrap inside to front, then around the outside to the back.

Knowledge and good, workable equipment will help ensure your horse's safety in and out of the trailer.

ensure proper ventilation, and it should have good padding on the floor. Foam or carpet pads under the rubber mats can provide extra cushion and insulation.

Another way to provide extra cushion and absorption is to put shavings on the floor of the trailer. The shavings also encourage the horse to urinate while traveling, because they reduce splash. Spray the shavings with mineral oil to prevent excessive dust in the trailer, which can contribute to respiratory problems.

Trailer safety is an important area of consideration. One way to help guard against accidents and injuries is to make sure that your horse is traveling in a safe trailer with a stout hitch. If you have any doubts about the safety of the rig, consult a horse trailer sales and service person.

In addition to checking the hitch, routinely check the floorboards of the trailer. This involves removing the mats to check

for rot, looking for any sharp objects, and checking for broken welds. Have the brakes checked and wheel bearings packed and greased by a knowledgeable mechanic. Examine and test the electrical system to avoid dangerous failures.

Be prepared for emergencies. I travel with a "vet kit"—a tackle box filled with a variety of first-aid materials that I can use in an emergency. This is not to be used in lieu of a veterinarian, but instead to help the horse until the veterinarian arrives. Talk to your veterinarian about what you should include in your vet kit and how to use/administer its contents. In addition to the vet kit, your knowledge about common illnesses and injuries, first-aid techniques for controlling bleeding and stabilizing injuries, and your horse's vital signs will be critical in an emergency situation.

Once the horse is loaded and you're en route, plan rest stops. On long trips, I

Before you run, check your equipment for loose screws, broken fasteners, etc., to prevent equipment failures from sabotaging your run.

Clean your horse's feet to remove built-up dirt, rocks, and other debris, and to check the condition of his shoes..

advise stopping every four to six hours. When you stop, find a safe place to unload and offer your horse water. If your horse has been trained, loading and unloading will not involve any extra stress.

When you arrive at your destination, your first consideration is the horse. Check him for injuries or signs of illness before putting him in his stall to rest. Check the stall for sharp objects or old feed that should be removed. Then allow your horse to rest, drink, and relax after the trailer ride.

Plan to arrive at the performance one to two hours prior to the competition. This gives you time to prepare a warm-up strategy. When you go to the office to pay your entry fee, pick up a day sheet (program insert) with the schedule of events. Also find out the order in which you run. This will help you "guesstimate" when you will run and when you need to warm

up, so you can be ready when it's your turn. This is all part of being prepared.

Arena Conditions

Unfortunately, there are some ground and arena situations that are conducive for hitting barrels. Deep, sandy ground can slow a horse down; barrels set close to fences can inhibit the momentum of the run and cause a lack of impulsion around a barrel. It takes an aggressive rider to get through this type of course.

In this arena situation, think about riding hard in order to maintain momentum through the entire run. The more momentum you can build, the better your chances of getting through the course without a barrel penalty. With the barrels close to the fences, the instant you sit to cue your horse to rate and turn, he'll see

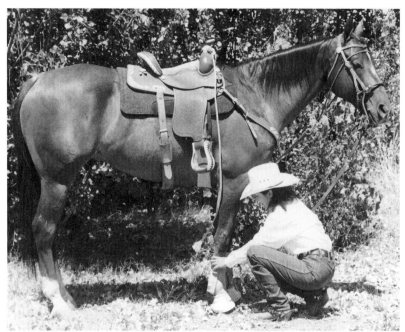

Put on your horse's protective leg gear.

When it is your turn to run, be mentally prepared to compete.

Remember: If ground conditions are not ideal, let your horse set the pace. In most cases horses will avoid the possibility of hurting themselves if they sense insecure footing.

The Warm-Up

The warm-up period can make or break the run. All horses need to be warmed or limbered up before competition, and some need to be mentally ridden down. A younger horse may need more loping than an older seasoned horse. It's important to know your horse well enough to identify when he's limber enough to compete.

Getting your horse to listen or pay attention to cues helps let you know when he is peaked and ready to make his best run. A good way to determine this is to time your warm-up and determine how long it takes him to reach his peak for competitive excellence. It is also important for the rider to be physically and mentally prepared to aid the horse in making his best possible run.

I consider an average warm-up time to be 45 minutes. Again this time can vary among horses. Nearly 35 of the 45 minutes will be spent walking. I walk my horses until they urinate, since this is my personal sign in the routine that tells me I can proceed with my warm-up. Other horses will have other signs that show you they're ready to proceed with their warm-up. It is up to you to learn to identify these consistent signs in your horse.

From the walk, jog for about five minutes to settle the horse's mind. If the horse feels flat, post a long trot to extend his stride and liven his attitude. Toward the end of that period I like to incorporate exercises that will help the horse become limber and respond to cues I give him in his run. For example, the figure-eight exercise will help limber the shoulder and at the same time remind him to move off the rein and balance his shoulder.

Lope for approximately 100 yards on each lead to loosen tendons and ligaments.

the closeness of the fence, and may turn too early, possibly slicing or hitting the barrel. Focus on second-cone position to overcome the urge to sit and rate too early.

A similar situation can occur in indoor conditions. When the horse feels a little more closed in, he has a tendency to perform a little more collected. It takes an intelligent rider to adjust the plan and make consistent, penalty-free runs in tight courses, because everything has a tendency to happen quicker.

Enter the arena beforehand, if possible, to identify ground conditions. Is the ground hard and slick, or deep and sticky, or just right? Understanding ground conditions and the size of the arena will help you establish a competitive "home court" advantage and a run strategy.

You may need to change your headgear or game plan to fit the arena conditions. Deep ground may mean you need a bit with less rate control, adjusted rate points, and more aggressive riding. Hard ground may mean you need increased control, a precise rate point, and the need to maintain a balanced horse. Being prepared before you go into competition will help you build the confidence necessary to achieve successful, consistent performances.

Loosen your cinch and lift up the back of the saddle and saddlepad to allow air to circulate. Adjust the saddle position if needed.

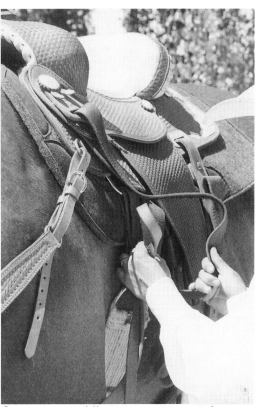

Once your saddle is in position, tighten the cinch.

Sprinting can come into play here to blow a horse for 30 yards or so. I also like to check my brakes. It never hurts to stop a time or two and re-balance a horse with a stop or rollback. At the completion of the warm-up the horse's attention must be on the rider.

It's important to prepare the horse for competition both mentally and physically. The more complete the warm-up, the more productive and consistent the run.

Plan to have the warm-up completed approximately 15 minutes before your run. While the horse relaxes check his feet for small rocks and packed dirt, check your equipment for potential weakness or worn spots, put on the horse's protective boots, and reset your saddle. Use this time to visualize your run. These are important parts of consistent pregame rituals. Tighten the cinch, mount, and prepare to make your run. Rubber bands can help you avoid losing your stirrups, yet will break easily in the event of an accident.

There is nothing worse than being late to compete, but if I find I've started the warm-up too soon I'll just stop and sit for a few minutes before continuing on. I don't want to warm the horse past his peak or to the point where he begins to flatten out and lose his competitive edge. Finding a good place to warm up can be difficult, but do the best you can. All too often the only place to warm up is a road or parking lot behind the arena. Be creative. Warm-up space is limited, so do as much walking as possible to keep the horse limber before a run.

The Run

When it is your turn to run, be mentally prepared to compete. Before the event you should have already picked your pocket points and your start points for your best approach. My main thought going to the first barrel is to ride aggressively to my preplanned position. Building momentum will create a quick turn and help with an effective rate. A successful first barrel sets

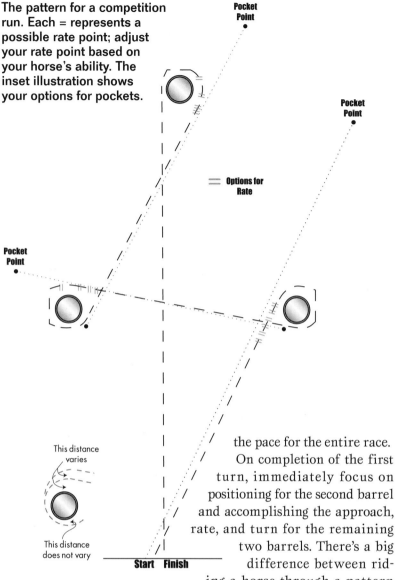

The pattern for a competition run. Each = represents a possible rate point; adjust your rate point based on your horse's ability. The inset illustration shows your options for pockets.

Pocket Point

Pocket Point

Pocket Point

= **Options for Rate**

This distance varies

This distance does not vary

Start   Finish

the pace for the entire race. On completion of the first turn, immediately focus on positioning for the second barrel and accomplishing the approach, rate, and turn for the remaining two barrels. There's a big difference between riding a horse through a pattern for training purposes and riding to win. In competition a well-trained horse should be relied on to do his part.

After the run, during my cool-out, I visualize the *feel* of my run, like an instant replay, to help identify my strengths and weaknesses. My run will be a report card that will help dictate my riding and training program between competitions.

Don't Beat Yourself

When arriving at a competition, try not to be too concerned with checking the existing times of any barrel racers who have gone before you. Barrel racing is so

competitive that you have to make a whale of a run regardless of what the other competitors have done.

Do not beat yourself. Your job is to make your best run by planning the run and running the plan. There are a number of barrel racers, at any time in any competition, who are capable of making a great run. Your focus should be placed on making your good, consistent run—then it's out of your hands and up to the rest of the competition to beat it.

The Competition

I like tough competition because it brings out the best in my personal performance. If you go into a race and know it's going to be tough to win, you should be ready to ride as aggressively as you can; if you expect to win, you have no other choice. Remember each competition should be treated as a report card and used as a resource to build a consistent and successful reputation.

Avoid paying too much attention to all the competitors entered in a barrel race. There will be only a few riders whose performance you'll really want to emulate. I like to watch talented riders on good horses make precise runs. This helps me visualize positive performance. Watching poor performance plants a negative picture and does not aid in creating productive competition. This practice is especially important for young riders; it helps prevent them from getting psyched out.

Don't allow yourself to be intimidated! Rookies and young riders need to remember that every champion started someplace. Go make the run you've prepared for, the good run you've visualized hundreds of times prior to competition, the same good run you have practiced at home. If competitors can't duplicate the same good runs at a competition that they're capable of making at home, they need to ask why.

Take the opportunity to watch top competitors. Watch how they handle their horses, how they prepare to make their runs, and what they do with their

Hooking a rubber band around your toe and heel (or spur) can help prevent the loss of your stirrup during a competition run. The rubber band will break if you get into trouble and need to get out of your saddle quickly (for example, if your horse falls).

Find a quiet spot and visualize your game plan: the approach, rate, and turn for each barrel. Relax, and be ready when it's your turn to run.

horses after their runs. Most champions are very gracious in sharing advice if asked at an appropriate time. Successful competition requires multidimensional resources. Seeking and refining information is a valuable resource for any budding competitor.

Confidence should override nervousness by way of the quality of your training and preparation. We all get nervous, but it's a skill to learn to channel the adrenaline in the favor of productive competition.

Greg Ward of Tulare, Calif., the late, great cow horse and cutting horse trainer, told me something I've never forgotten: "You can go and worry about the competition, and worry whether your horse will work, or whether you've selected the right bridle. But if you've done your homework, you should be able to go out and just enjoy your ride."

I agree. All your hard work and effort is not worth it if you can't have fun.

In Perspective

My first book was written during the time when my focus was competition. The word "I" was predominant.

Today, the competitive arena is no longer my focus. This book has evolved from our clinic program and focuses on education; a consistent and successful approach to the diligent process of training, conditioning, and nutrition; and well-planned and organized competition. My goal is that it teaches each reader to enjoy the process, in order to make successful competition a personal art form.

SURVEY OF WINNERS

A dozen of the sport's great riders and their horses.

NEW COMPETITORS who begin to experience the confidence produced by winning runs often believe that they have found the key to training successful barrel horses. If they have the opportunity to stay in the profession long enough, they begin to learn that the search for replacement prospects eventually has a

Charmayne James has set an unprecedented record of 17 NFR qualifications including 10 world titles won with her great horse Scamper, shown here. Most impressive is Charmayne's ability to allow her horses to perform to their full potential by riding relaxed and balanced. Charmayne has impressed her fans by demonstrating her winning skills on a number of horses. She is a poised competitor and a gracious champion. Charmayne's ability as a trainer is becoming highly respected.

KENNETH SPRINGER

By SPRINGER

way of humbling even the most talented of trainers.

I modify my expectations according to the individual horse's attitude, desire, and ability. There have been times I have even thrown up my hands wondering what to try next; I have exhausted all my knowledge. I am, however, stimulated and encouraged when I think of the number of horses I have seen respond to the basic theories and principles of balanced horsemanship reiterated in this book.

Good horses in any equestrian discipline are a gift. Few champions have the opportunity to experience more than one great horse in a lifetime. Though individual breeding offers little guarantee, one thing these great equine athletes have in common is athletic ability, an abundance of quick speed, and—most important—the desire to excel under a variety of challenging conditions.

Once these rare individuals are discovered, it then becomes the responsibility of the rider to develop and nurture these qualities. The horse and rider establish a bond of respect and a confidence that develops through consistent, productive training and competition.

Great horses give good riders a chance to become great horsemen. The following riders have demonstrated their ability to enhance their horses' performance through effective horsemanship and balanced riding techniques.

By SPRINGER

KENNETH SPRINGER

Jimmie Munroe is a past world champion; a talented, multidimensional horsewoman; and a gracious wife and mother. Jimmie's consistent abilities qualified her for 11 NFR competitions, and her management and leadership skills enabled her, as WPRA president for an unprecedented 15 years, to direct the WPRA into the respected organization it is today. Jimmie depends on horsemanship skills for consistency and longevity on the horses she rides.

Martha Josey is the competitor's competitor and has mastered the art of sports psychology. She holds the distinction of earning the WPRA world championship and the AQHA world championship the same year, 1980, aboard Sonny Bit O Both. Her longevity and ability to identify world-class horses (like Orange Smash, her mount in this photo) has allowed her to qualify for the NFR for four decades. I salute Martha for her love of the sport and her insatiable appetite for excellence.

Another WPRA world champion, Sherry Cervi has the confidence to draw on her horsemanship skills to excel on a number of talented horses. She impresses me with her ability to remain balanced and poised under the strenuous circumstances involved with professional competition. Sherry is a true athlete who uses her competitive intuition in selecting which of her horses she feels have the ability to excel best under different conditions. Sherry's versatility allows her to modify her successful game plan to utilize incremental conditions in her favor.

Carol Goostree, 1979 WPRA world champion, respects the resource of horsemanship and shares in my belief that a solid training foundation is important to the success and longevity of any talented prospect. In addition to training her great horse Dobre, Carol has helped qualify two other barrel racers for the NFR on three of the horses she has personally trained.

I respect Kristie Peterson not only for her horsemanship talents but also for the poise and gracious attitude that has gained this multi-time world champion respect in the equine industry. Kristie has demonstrated her ability to see the potential in her great horse Bozo, shown here. Not only did she train him herself, but she also had the ability to identify and adapt her riding style to allow Bozo to mature into the respected world-class athlete he is today.

Multi-time NFR-qualifier and reserve world champion Kay Blandford is known for her aggressive attitude and her competitive passion. When Kay wins she makes everybody around her feel like they have won too. Here she is riding The Key Grip, a 15.1, 1,200-pound halter-bred gelding affectionately known as Llave. During a three-year dominance, Llave earned more at the prestigious Old Fort Days Futurity and Derby in Fort Smith, Ark., than most horses win in a lifetime. The little horse with a big heart has won close to half a million dollars.

Lynn McKenzie recognized the potential of her great horse Magnolia Missle early on. Missle was one of the first of many great futurity winners to excel in professional competition by winning two world titles. I had the opportunity to ride Missle once—it was a thrill I will never forget. Missle was a balanced athlete with the ability to excel under a variety of circumstances.

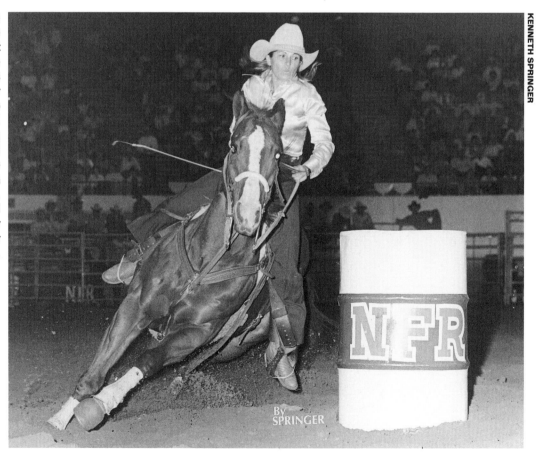

KENNETH SPRINGER

Talmadge Green was the first competitor to win $2,000,000 in barrel racing competition. Talmadge has the unique ability to adapt his riding skills to incorporate the style of many different horses. He is an aggressive, focused competitor who has a great ability to locate and develop promising prospects. The majority of Talmadge's earnings has been in futurity and derby competitions.

KENNETH SPRINGER

Deb Mohon rides her great horse Brown. Voted Horse With The Most Heart by the WPRA's top 15, Brown qualified Deb for 11 NFRs and won the reserve world championship title in 1990. This was an exciting pair to watch, as demonstrated in this photo taken at Cheyenne where Brown gives his all in the deep ground. Consistency is a strong motivator, and Brown made every run count.

Dale Youree was one of the first men to enter barrel racing competitions. Dale and his wife, Florence, former Girls Rodeo Association all-around world champion, have remained influential trainers, competitors, and clinicians for over 40 years. Dale and Florence were instrumental in establishing the barrel horse futurity industry that we know today.

Mildred Farris qualified for 11 NFRs, and her consistent performance won her 4 reserve world championships. Mildred was not only a great competitor but also served as WPRA president for 10 years. I respect Mildred for her gracious presence and her ability to be a tough competitor, a businesswoman, and a lady all at the same time.

Three winners—Sharon, Super Stick, and Seven—enjoying quieter times after years of successful competition.

PROFILE: SHARON CAMARILLO

By Kendra Santos

WHEN SHARON Camarillo—then Sharon Avril Meffan—was just a 3-year-old half-pint, a pony-tailed pipsqueak making her Saturday morning rounds on rented ponies in picturesque Redondo Beach, Calif., she didn't look all that much different than other kids. They were smiling in the saddle on the rented ponies too. The difference was, one ride was enough for them. Riding was a kick, but no bigger

Sharon and Seven at their first National Finals Rodeo— Oklahoma City, December 1979.

KENNETH SPRINGER

thrill than splashing in the waves and building sand castles. And "horse" wasn't one of their first words.

Even then, when it came to horses, Sharon was different. She couldn't get enough time in the saddle. And the typical pony wasn't good enough. She didn't figure she'd gotten her money's worth until she got those ponies to pick up the pace and trot.

A few blocks away, Bob and Avril Meffan raised Sharon and her little brother, Kenneth, who grew up to be an accomplished architect, in a middle-class residential neighborhood. Bob made a significant contribution to the U.S. space program as an aeronautical engineer at Northrup Aviation, which was located near their home in the suburbs of Los Angeles. Avril was a model wife and mother, a skilled baker and seamstress who stylishly yet thriftily outfitted her kids with her handiwork.

They were a happy family that enjoyed camping and fishing—anything they did together, really.

"As time has passed, I've realized how special that lifestyle was," Sharon now reflects. "It was like days gone by. The children were the focal point of the family. My mom was at home full time, and my dad worked in the aeronautical industry for 45 years. It was a childhood full of stability and traditions, the epitome of the postwar, baby-boomer environment, with the big tree at Christmas and an Easter basket on Easter morning."

Sharon had just one complaint: She didn't have a horse of her own in the backyard, and those six days between Saturdays seemed like six years.

This is not your typical city-girl-makes-good story. It's proof that dreams really do come true when smart choices are made, goals are set from the heart, and determination is genuine.

The chances that this little blond beach bunny—who could sniff out the horses from a mile away on her family's trips into the Sierra Mountains, Mammoth Lakes, Big Bear Lake, or Yosemite, and

Increasingly busy with clinics and rodeo commentating, Sharon still likes spending quiet time horseback.

who kept a horse brush in her bedroom because she loved the smell of a horse— would someday earn guru status in the western world were way beyond unlikely.

"I would smell manure or find a piece of barbed wire and think, 'There's a horse around here somewhere,' " she remembers. "My grandmother lived 30 miles away in Montebello, which was rural country. We'd drive out there on Sundays, and I was obsessed with trying to spot horses.

Sharon's family established her love for the outdoors very early in life.

Sharon was born a California city girl.

"I was a city girl with a country heart. I just knew I'd rather be poor and live in the country than be rich in the city. Early on I sensed where my love lay, and I was so lucky to have the support of my family."

Some family friends owned a livestock auction in nearby San Jacinto, where Sharon spent her Saturdays after she outgrew the ponies at the beach. She cut cattle and herded them into the sale ring from horseback. From then on, she was torn between the family's weekend expeditions and the sale barn. When she did head for the hills with her family, she envied the perks of the forest rangers. Sharon observed that they lived in the country and had access to all kinds of horses—it looked inviting. By 12, however, she was pretty sure the cattle buyer/auctioneer combination she saw at the sales yard was her calling.

"About that time, my dad took me to the (1962) National Finals Rodeo in Los

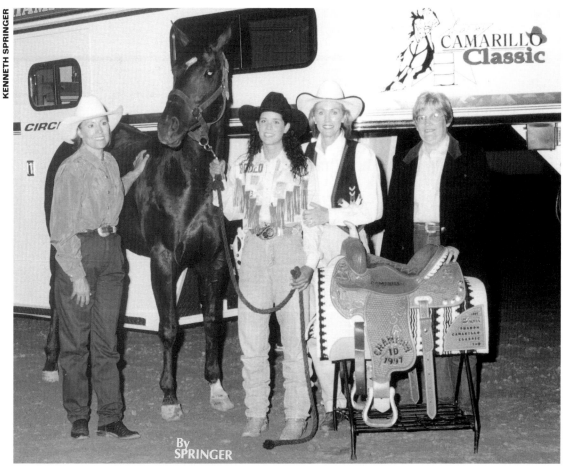

KENNETH SPRINGER

The annual Sharon Camarillo Classic is a competition where students of Sharon's clinics can put to the test what they've learned. In this photo Sharon presents Marvel Murphy with her awards for winning the 1997 event. Also pictured are Shirley Ankrum, clinic instructor, and Deb Wood, manager of the Classic.

Angeles," she remembers. "We had top row seats, way up high. I wore a new white jeans-and-jacket outfit that I'd bought by saving my allowance. When I saw the barrel race, I was hooked. As a naive child, I saw rodeo as a glamorous extension of the ranch way of life, which I loved. I loved the riding, the cattle, and the horsemanship."

At home, she loved to watch old westerns. She saw a role model in Dale Evans. "She was a cowgirl, but she also had a family and a career, a strong career, while always maintaining her femininity and individualism," Camarillo said.

Sounds familiar. It's a description that would also come to fit Camarillo. But first, the foundation—a solid education.

Growing Up

"College was not optional in my house," she said with an appreciative smile. "But,

of course, I automatically looked for an agricultural college."

After graduating from Aviation High School in 1966, Sharon attended Pierce Junior College in California's San Fernando Valley on a rodeo scholarship. Two years later, armed with an associate's degree in agricultural business, she headed up the coast to San Luis Obispo, where she enrolled at California Polytechnic State University. Another couple years of studying hard at the famous rodeo school best known as "Cal Poly" earned Sharon a bachelor's degree in business administration and a minor in agriculture.

She always enjoyed running barrels. But Sharon excelled in breakaway roping and goat tying at the college level because she could compensate for her lack of horsepower (she couldn't afford a good horse) with endless hours of ground-work. While the other girls slept, she roped a

En route to the first of four NFR qualifications: Sharon and Seven at the 1979 Houston Livestock Show Rodeo.

KENNETH SPRINGER

dummy and tied her practice goats.

Her diligence paid off with a National Intercollegiate Rodeo Association national goat tying championship. Sharon also won regional goat tying and all-around titles, and did Dale Evans proud by finishing first runner-up in the Miss College Rodeo pageant, which was based on poise, appearance, and horsemanship.

"When I graduated from college, I realized that if I wanted to stay involved with rodeo, the barrel race was my resource," she remembers. "I went to the all-girl rodeos that summer. That's when I first

started trying to make a barrel horse."

She went to work as a flight attendant for a major airline, and enjoyed the flexibility the schedule allowed. "I rode with the telephone placed outside, and if the airline called me to work, I was within an hour of the airport," she said. "Just think what I could have done with a cellular phone!"

Sharon especially enjoyed the extended leaves allowed in that line of work, because she found it tough to be competitive when she couldn't keep her horses on a consistent training schedule.

Sharon's family is an important part of her life. Here's the whole bunch: parents Bob and Avril Meffan, son Wade, Sharon, daughter Storme, and Leo Camarillo.

Mrs. Camarillo

Miss Meffan met Leo Camarillo in the spring of the year when she was 27, at the Chowchilla (Calif.) Stampede. They were married that November.

They don't call Leo "The Lion" for nothing. He's a fierce competitor, an all-around timed-event great who owned the arena for decades and revolutionized team roping. Leo won world team roping titles in 1972, '73, '75, and '83. He won the PRCA championship in 1976, one of three years the world title was based only on sudden-death NFR earnings. In 1975, the ProRodeo Hall of Famer sat atop rodeo's ultimate throne as the world champion all-around cowboy.

Leo still holds the record for most NFR team roping average titles. He won the Finals with Billy Wilson in 1968; with his cousin, Reg Camarillo, in '69, '70, and '71; and in '80 and '82 with Tee Woolman.

Marrying Leo was a milestone in Sharon's life. It was also a turning point in her career, when barrel racing shifted gears for Sharon, and she took her competitive edge to a new level.

Her experience in the rodeo world makes Sharon an ideal commentator at many events, such as the Houston Livestock Show and Rodeo, where she posed with a Longhorn friend.

"I had the opportunity to take Leo's calf horse, Charlie, who'd had some futurity experience, and run him," she said. "Charlie was the first really nice horse I got to ride."

She qualified Charlie for the Sierra Circuit Finals, and Sharon and the cute little bay horse went on to run consistently with the world-class field.

That experience led to Sharon's greatest competitive triumph—four straight National Finals Rodeo qualifications on a super horse she trained herself. She called him Seven.

"I've always said the proudest moment of my life was having the opportunity to ride with my husband in that first grand entry at the (1979) National Finals Rodeo," she says. "I'd accomplished a major goal. I ran the fastest time at that first NFR I went to, but that didn't mean as much to me."

After that first NFR, Sharon set out to learn to ride "technically correctly." She noticed that many horses on the rodeo road lacked strong fundamental foundations, and she figured there must be a better way.

With that in mind, Sharon and Seven stormed the country, winning major rodeos from coast to coast and a state championship. When Seven hurt himself late in the season one year, Sharon cowgirled up, went on with it, and qualified for the NFR on a borrowed mare. But once she'd "been there and done that," it was time to make another move.

Time for a Change

"I'm so goal-oriented that once the goal is achieved, it's checked off and filed—it's history," she said. "After that fourth NFR (in 1982) I stepped back and decided I really wanted to learn to ride, and how to communicate with and train horses. I'd achieved some successes and accomplished some goals because of my natural competitive instincts, but I had the opportunity to ride with some very successful trainers and learn the ABCs of horsemanship.

"Barrel racing was still my main love, but I experienced things with reined cow horses, cutting horses, and dressage that I could apply to barrel racing. I showed both Seven and Charlie in reined cow horse contests. I did it to prove to myself that I could be respected by my peers in other equestrian disciplines."

By then Sharon had developed a theory about goals, and realized the power of long-term, mid-range, and short-term goal-setting. Long-term goals are the ultimate; the others are the stepping stones on the path to getting there.

"I always emphasize goal-setting, because it's how I've lived my life," she said. "It's very important that goals are realistic, believable, and achievable. To set them, you need to determine your weaknesses, recognize your strengths, and seek solutions. We all have different goals, but the formula is the same. Goals are important because they keep you disciplined, focused, and in a positive direction to build confidence.

"I realized that I wanted longevity in this business, and that I didn't want to be

In 1997 Sharon received the Tad Lucas Award at the Cowboy Hall of Fame in Oklahoma City. The award recognizes "the contribution of women in the field of rodeo as well as the western industry in and out of the arena."

judged on the last run I made. So I made a plan for getting where I wanted to go. As I look back, I'm so thankful for the lifestyle I've created for myself. I now realize how critical productive choices are from an early age, because everything I did along the way is what got me here. Every stage of life is a choice, and the key to success is making good, educated choices."

The way Sharon sees it, integrity, honesty, and self-esteem are the foundations of self-confidence. "It all boils down to liking yourself," she stated simply.

Sharon and Bob Feist at the Sharon Camarillo Classic.

KENNETH SPRINGER

Life Today

Leo and Sharon welcomed their son, Wade, into the world on Christmas Eve, 1986. "Wade's been the biggest blessing of my life," she says. "He's allowed me to experience more emotions in life and has taught me about unconditional love. He's my No. 1 goal now. He's seen 38 states and 2 space shuttle launches. He's interested in aviation, which follows in my dad's footsteps."

Sharon is raising Wade with the values that have taken her to the top of her professions, because she feels those character-building traits will help Wade succeed in whatever he decides to pursue.

Sharon's juggling act is familiar to many modern-day American career women. In addition to her roles as mother to Wade and adopted daughter Storme, Camarillo is a clinician, endorsee, clothing designer, competition coach, horsemanship instructor, author, commentator, and television personality.

Sharon's endless assets were recognized in 1997 when she was named the Tad Lucas Award winner by the National Cowboy Hall of Fame and Western Heritage Center in Oklahoma City. Lucas was a world champion all-around cowgirl in the "golden cowgirl era" of the early 1900s. The Tad Lucas Award recognizes "the contribution of women in the field of rodeo as well as the western industry in and out of the arena." The bronze medal is presented annually by Lucas' daughter, Mitzi Riley.

"Our success is only limited by the scope of our dreams," Sharon said at the Hall of Fame podium. "We should never be afraid to excel or stand up for what we believe."

Professionalism, dignity, and grace characterize every aspect of the multi-dimensional, contemporary western woman. Sharon's barrel racing and horsemanship clinic students become friends and fans, because they have her sincere support. And she grows as an instructor daily, because she's constantly processing and analyzing new information.

Camarillo has shared that wealth of

information with students from each end of the competitive spectrum and all points in between: NFR-qualifiers to 65-year-old grandmothers just struggling for the courage to enter. She established the Sharon Camarillo Classic, a premier barrel racing event reserved for her students, to give aspiring barrel racers from every level a chance to showcase their talents and further develop themselves as competitors. The fitting motto of the event: "Look for the star in you."

"We have a responsibility to look inside ourselves and be realistic about what we want," she said. "It all goes back to goals and choices. We all need to take responsibility for establishing our goals. If we don't do it, who will? Challenges give us a chance to grow and cultivate new resources, and there's a reward in overcoming challenges. It's a process that builds strength and character.

"I'm an eternal horsemanship student," she said. "I tell people, 'I'm here in defense of your horses.' People need to communicate better with their horses. The answer is not a bigger whip or sharper spurs, or avoiding knowledge and skills and just hoping you'll stumble onto the right horse that will magically perform perfectly despite you. Horses are not disposable, and you owe it to your horse to make him the best he can be."

So many of her theories were sparked back in the days she and Leo zigzagged the map to rodeos everywhere, including the Presidential Rodeo in Washington, D.C., in 1983, and a Wrangler-sponsored rodeo tour of Argentina. Sharon travels extensively with her clinics and horse fairs, which have taken her to many countries, including Australia and Germany.

The Camarillos' career paths have forked a bit, but they continue to recognize and respect each other's achievements. They've always been driven by a desire to top their personal best that motivates them to never quit striving for more. It's a trait they share with winners from all walks of life.

"I have an innate instinct to survive

"I'm an eternal horsemanship student," Sharon says. "People need to communicate better with their horses. You owe it to your horse to make him the best he can be."

and excel, but Leo came along and gave me the resources to succeed," Sharon says gratefully. "He taught me how to enter and travel, and let me on that first good horse. But more importantly, he set a high example for me to follow."

Kendra Santos, the former editor of PRCA's ProRodeo Sports News *and current editor-in-chief of PBR's* Pro Bull Rider, *lives in Creston, California.*

GLOSSARY

Aids: The signals a rider uses to communicate and request movements from the horse. Natural aids include the rider's voice, legs, seat, and hands. Artificial aids include bats, spurs, over-and-unders, and martingales.

Approach: The mechanical process of guiding a horse in balanced position into the rating position of a barrel. The proper balanced approach will help promote successful rate and turn.

Arc: In the context of barrel racing, arc refers to the flexible "bending" desired in barrel racing horses during a turn around a barrel. The horse's body literally forms a slight curve from nose through poll, shoulder, and loin, as he shows free-flowing movement in front and behind. The inside hock reaches up and across the outside hock in such a turn.

Average: Competitions with more than one go-round pay prize money for each round, plus money for the best average, or total time. In such a competition, the winner of the average is the overall winner of the contest.

Collection: Refers to the horse's ability to shorten the length of his stride at each gait and includes a shortening of the horse's overall body length.

Diagonal: A term used to refer to the rider's ability, at the trot, to rise and sit (post) in time with the horse's stride, rising as the horse's outside shoulder is up and sitting when that same shoulder is down, or when that foreleg hits the ground. The trot is a two-beat gait where the horse's legs move in diagonal pairs, separated by a moment of suspension. A phrase to help remember which diagonal is correct is "rise and fall with shoulder on the wall."

Direct rein: Use of the rein to indicate same-side control. If a turn to the right is desired, the right-hand rein will be used to direct, by gentle pulling, the horse's head to the right.

Extension: Refers to the horse's stride being as long as possible with hindquarters fully engaged. The horse remains calm and light on the forehand. Strides are lowered and lengthened versus being elevated and quick.

Frame: A term used to describe the practice of creating and maintaining a balanced horse, both side to side and front to back. It involves the rider using correct rein and leg aids to control and isolate each part of the horse's body.

Indirect rein: In this context, it is the opposite of the direct rein. While the direct rein controls the direction of the front end, the indirect rein controls and stabilizes the outside shoulder and hind leg.

Impulsion: It is contained energy, and should not be confused with speed. Impulsion is initiated by the hindquarters and allows the horse the power to go forward as soon as the rider requests.

Lead: Term referring to the sequence of legs leaving the ground at the canter or lope. There is a left lead and a right lead. The canter is a three-beat gait with a moment of suspension when all four feet are off the ground. The rider can determine the lead by observing and determining which foreleg is the last leg to hit the ground in the sequence. In the right lead, for example, the sequence would be left hind leg, right hind leg and left foreleg together, then right foreleg, followed by a moment of suspension.

Pocket: The turning area between horse and barrel. This area varies among individual horses.

Pocket point: A point, identified with a visual landmark, that assists in identifying the correct distance from each barrel to approach the pocket. Adjustments are made based on the individual horse's level of training and the horse's athletic ability to maneuver the turn. **Key:** The horse must be positioned in the pocket to allow him to leave the barrel close.

Propping: A term used to describe the horse becoming extremely heavy on the forehand in a rate or stop. The rider generally is "propped" out of the saddle as a result of the rough transition.

Range of vision: Looking ahead to the point of the circle where the horse is aimed. Use a longer range, 25 feet, for larger circles and a shorter range, 3 feet, for a barrel turn.

Rate: In barrel racing, rate is the maneuver in which the horse shortens or adjusts his stride in order to prepare for a barrel turn.

Rate point: A point at each barrel where the rider will request the horse to rate. Adjustments are made based on arena configurations and the requirements of each individual horse.

Shoulder elevation: the process of lifting a horse's shoulder to a balanced, framed body position.

Shoulder/hip correction: A maneuver to help lift and rebalance the horse's ribcage. "Shoulder/hip" describes the leg movement of the rider as the horse is bumped in the shoulder to lift and then bumped in the rear cinch area to drive forward.

Slicing: This is caused by the horse attempting to turn a barrel too soon, when the hip slings out and the shoulder drops in. Slicing results in either a knocked down barrel or improper turn, either of which can cause the horse to be out of position for the approach to the next barrel.

Start point: A point identified with a visual landmark that assists in determining the correct place to begin the approach to the first barrel. Adjustments are made based on arena configurations and requirements of each individual horse.

ORGANIZATIONS

BARREL RACING courses vary, and for that reason so do winning times, depending on the size of arenas and ground conditions. For pattern regulations, additional rules, and general information, contact these associations:

Women's Professional Rodeo Association
1235 Lake Plaza Drive, Suite 134
Colorado Springs, CO 80906
719-576-0900
www.wpra.com

American Quarter Horse Association
Box 200
Amarillo, TX 79168
806-376-4811
www.aqha.com

National Barrel Horse Association
1355 Reynolds
Augusta, GA 30901-1050
706-722-7223
www.nbha.com

American Paint Horse Association
Box 961023
Fort Worth, TX 76161-0023
www.apha.com

American West 4D
1313 S. Blaker Road
Turlock, CA 95380
209-667-6019
www.americanwest4d.com

Nas Horse Racing
5311A Wares Ferry Road
Montgomery, AL 36109
334-409-9905
www.nashorse.com

Barrel Futurities of America
4701 Parsons Road
Springdale, AR 72764
www.barrelhorses.com/BFA

For additional educational information and schedules of the Sharon Camarillo clinic program, contact her Web-site at **www.sharoncamarillo.com**.

THANK YOU

SHARON CAMARILLO would like to thank these friends and sponsors:

American Hat Company, Conroe, Texas

Ariat Boot Company, San Carlos, California

Jimmy and Kathy Court of Courts Saddlery, Bryan, Texas

Farnam Companies Inc., Phoenix, Arizona

Bob Brandon, Glen and John Taylor, and
Larry and Brenda Sargent of Reinsman Equestrian Products, Inc., Cleveland, Tennessee

Purina Mills, Inc.

Wrangler, Greensboro, North Carolina

Dr. David Hayes, D.V.M., Meridian, Idaho

Dennis Nissan, Acampo, California

Jim Price, Ridgefield, Washington

The *Western Horseman*, established in 1936, is the world's leading horse publication. For subscription information: 800-877-5278. To order other *Western Horseman* books: 800-874-6774. *Western Horseman*, Box 7980, Colorado Springs, CO 80933-7980. Web-site: **www.westernhorseman.com**.

Books Published by Western Horseman Inc.

ARABIAN LEGENDS by Marian K. Carpenter
280 pages and 319 photographs. Abu Farwa, *Aladdinn, *Ansata Ibn Halima, *Bask, Bay-Abi, Bay El Bey, Bint Sahara, Fadjur, Ferzon, Indraff, Khemosabi, *Morafic, *Muscat, *Naborr, *Padron, *Raffles, *Raseyn, *Sakr, Samtyr, *Sanacht, *Serafix, Skorage, *Witez II, Xenophonn.

BACON & BEANS by Stella Hughes
144 pages and 200-plus recipes for delicious western chow.

BARREL RACING, Completely Revised by Sharon Camarillo
128 pages, 158 photographs, and 17 illustrations. Teaches foundation horsemanship and barrel racing skills for horse and rider, with additional tips on feeding, hauling, and winning.

CALF ROPING by Roy Cooper
144 pages and 280 photographs covering roping and tying.

CUTTING by Leon Harrel
144 pages and 200 photographs. Complete guide on this popular sport.

FIRST HORSE by Fran Devereux Smith
176 pages, 160 black-and-white photos, about 40 illustrations. Step-by-step information for the first-time horse owner and/or novice rider.

HORSEMAN'S SCRAPBOOK by Randy Steffen
144 pages and 250 illustrations. A collection of handy hints.

IMPRINT TRAINING by Robert M. Miller, D.V.M.
144 pages and 250 photographs. Learn to "program" newborn foals.

LEGENDS by Diane C. Simmons
168 pages and 214 photographs. Barbra B, Bert, Chicaro Bill, Cowboy P-12, Depth Charge (TB), Doc Bar, Go Man Go, Hard Twist, Hollywood Gold, Joe Hancock, Joe Reed P-3, Joe Reed II, King P-234, King Fritz, Leo, Peppy, Plaudit, Poco Bueno, Poco Tivio, Queenie, Quick M Silver, Shue Fly, Star Duster, Three Bars (TB), Top Deck (TB), and Wimpy P-1.

LEGENDS 2 by Jim Goodhue, Frank Holmes, Phil ❦ Livingston, Diane C. Simmons
192 pages and 224 photographs. Clabber, Driftwood, Easy Jet, Grey Badger II, Jessie James, Jet Deck, Joe Bailey P-4 (Gonzales), Joe Bailey (Weatherford), King's Pistol, Lena's Bar, Lightning Bar, Lucky Blanton, Midnight, Midnight Jr, Moon Deck, My Texas Dandy, Oklahoma Star, Oklahoma Star Jr., Peter McCue, Rocket Bar (TB), Skipper W, Sugar Bars, and Traveler.

LEGENDS 3 by Jim Goodhue, Frank Holmes, Diane Ciarloni, Kim Guenther, Larry Thornton, Betsy Lynch
208 pages and 196 photographs. Flying Bob, Hollywood Jac 86, Jackstraw (TB), Maddon's Bright Eyes, Mr Gun Smoke, Old Sorrel, Piggin String (TB), Poco Lena, Poco Pine, Poco Dell, Question Mark, Quo Vadis, Royal King, Showdown, Steel Dust, and Two Eyed Jack.

LEGENDS 4
Several authors chronicle the great Quarter Horses Zantanon, Ed Echols, Zan Parr Bar, Blondy's Dude, Diamonds Sparkle, Woven Web/Miss Princess, Miss Bank, Rebel Cause, Tonto Bars Hank, Harlan, Lady Bug's Moon, Dash For Cash, Vandy, Impressive, Fillinic, Zippo Pine Bar, and Doc O' Lena.

LEGENDS 5 by Frank Holmes, Ty Wyant, Alan Gold, and Sally Harrison
The stories of Little Joe, Joe Moore, Monita, Bill Cody, Joe Cody, Topsail Cody, Pretty Buck, Pat Star Jr., Skipa Star, Hank H, Chubby, Bartender, Leo San, Custus Rastus (TB), Jaguar, Jackie Bee, Chicado V, and Mr Bar None fill 248 pages, including about 300 photographs.

PROBLEM-SOLVING by Marty Marten
248 pages and over 250 photos and illustrations. How to develop a willing partnership between horse and human to handle trailer-loading, hard-to-catch, barn-sour, spooking, water-crossing, herd-bound, and pull-back problems.

NATURAL HORSE-MAN-SHIP by Pat Parelli
224 pages and 275 photographs. Parelli's six keys to a natural horse-human relationship.

REINING, Completely Revised by Al Dunning
216 pages and over 300 photographs showing how to train horses for this exciting event.

RODEO LEGENDS by Gavin Ehringer
Photos and life stories fill 216 pages. Included are: Joe Alexander, Jake Barnes & Clay O'Brien Cooper, Joe Beaver, Leo Camarillo, Roy Cooper, Tom Ferguson, Bruce Ford, Marvin Garrett, Don Gay, Tuff Hedeman, Charmayne James, Bill Linderman, Larry Mahan, Ty Murray, Dean Oliver, Jim Shoulders, Casey Tibbs, Harry Tompkins, and Fred Whitfield.

ROOFS AND RAILS by Gavin Ehringer
144 pages, 128 black-and-white photographs plus drawings, charts, and floor plans. How to plan and build your ideal horse facility.

STARTING COLTS by Mike Kevil
168 pages and 400 photographs. Step-by-step process in starting colts.

THE HANK WIESCAMP STORY by Frank Holmes
208 pages and over 260 photographs. The biography of the legendary breeder of Quarter Horses, Appaloosas, and Paints.

TEAM PENNING by Phil Livingston
144 pages and 200 photographs. How to compete in this popular family sport.

TEAM ROPING WITH JAKE AND CLAY by Fran Devereux Smith
224 pages and over 200 photographs and illustrations. Learn about fast times from champions Jake Barnes and Clay O'Brien Cooper. Solid information about handling a rope, roping dummies, and heading and heeling for practice and in competition. Also sound advice about rope horses, roping steers, gear, and horsemanship.

WELL-SHOD by Don Baskins
160 pages, 300 black-and-white photos and illustrations. A horseshoeing guide for owners and farriers. The easy-to-read text, illustrations, and photos show step-by-step how to trim and shoe a horse for a variety of uses. Special attention is paid to corrective shoeing techniques for horses with various foot and leg problems.

WESTERN HORSEMANSHIP by Richard Shrake
144 pages and 150 photographs. Complete guide to riding western horses.

WESTERN TRAINING by Jack Brainard
With Peter Phinny. 136 pages. Stresses the foundation for western training.

WIN WITH BOB AVILA by Juli S. Thorson
This 128-page, hardbound, full-color book discusses traits that separate horse-world achievers from also-rans. World champion horseman Bob Avila shares his philosophies on succeeding as a competitor, breeder, and trainer.